IMAGES
of America

NEW YORK CITY GANGLAND

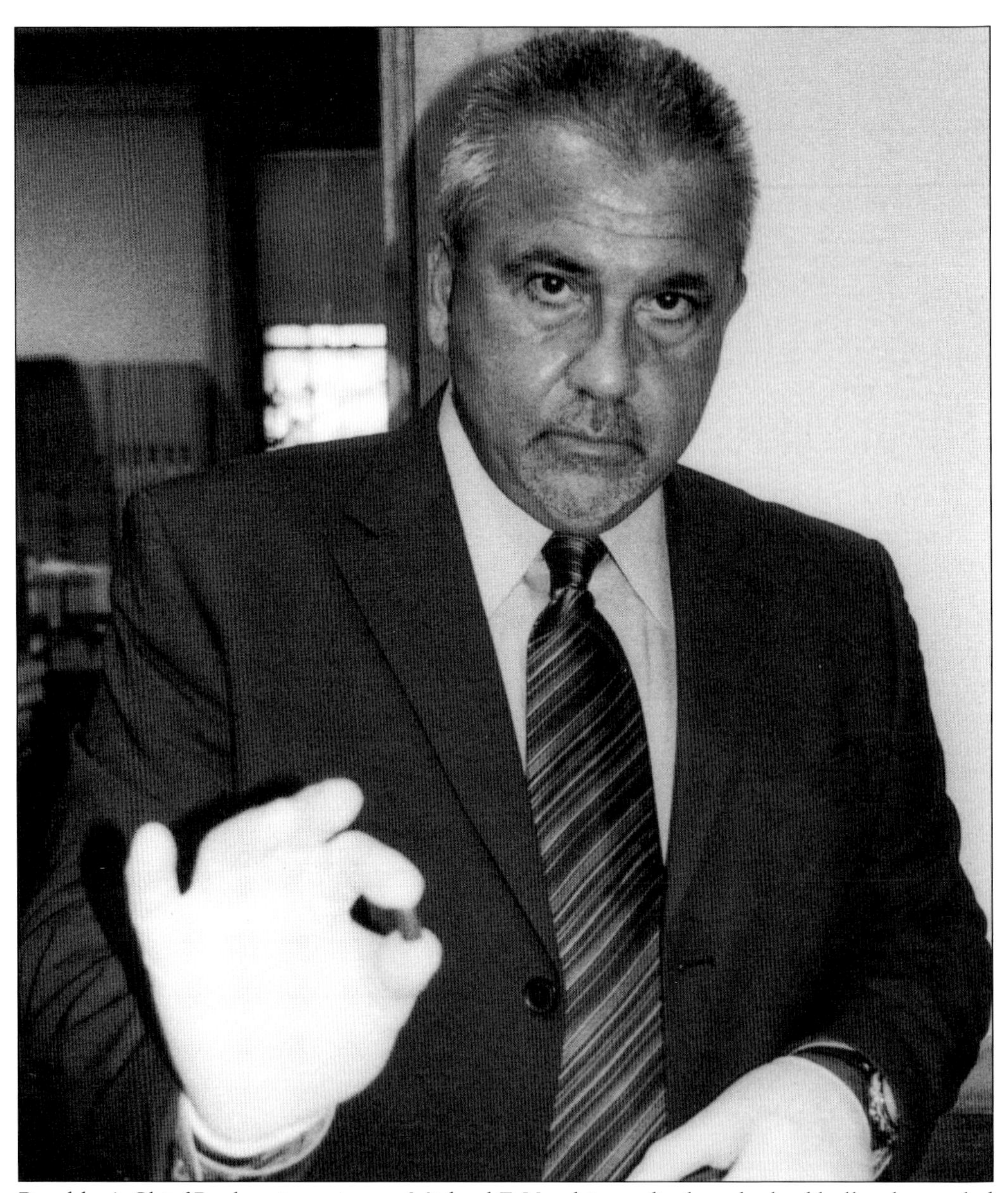

Brooklyn's Chief Rackets investigator, Michael F. Vecchione, displays the lead bullet that ended Ferdinand "The Shadow" Boccia in 1934 on the orders of Vito Genovese, who fled the United States to evade justice. When Genovese returned in 1946, the sole witness against him abruptly died. On the morning this image was taken, Vecchione began prosecuting a senior FBI operative accused of leaking confidential information to the Columbo crime family. (Photograph by Arthur Nash.)

On the Cover: The fedora-flaunting felons of "Murder, Inc." engage in an impromptu stare down with a New York Police Department (NYPD) photographer around 1933. A combination of less-than-kosher Jewish assassins and equally disreputable Italian triggermen, these thugs-for-hire settled hundreds of scores for the New York City underworld until their disintegration in 1940. For identifications see pages 42–43. (Author's collection.)

IMAGES
of America
NEW YORK CITY
GANGLAND

Arthur Nash

ARCADIA
PUBLISHING

ISBN 978-0-7385-7314-4

Published by Arcadia Publishing
Charleston, South Carolina

Printed in the United States of America

Library of Congress Control Number: 2009942704

For all general information contact Arcadia Publishing at:
Telephone 843-853-2070
Fax 843-853-0044
E-mail sales@arcadiapublishing.com
For customer service and orders:
Toll-Free 1-888-313-2665

Visit us on the Internet at www.arcadiapublishing.com

The author wishes to dedicate this collection in loving memory of Arthur Alan Weinstein Z'L, friend and mentor, King of the Night.

Contents

Acknowledgments

I am grateful to select contributors whose appreciation for history is rivaled only by their generosity. Thank you.

Avraham Bash; John J. Binder; Butch Aquilino; Selwyn Raab; Frederick T. Martens, PA Organized Crime Commission and NJ State Police; Michael F. Vecchione, Kings County (Brooklyn) Rackets chief; Leonora A. Gidlund, director of the Manhattan Municipal Archives; Joe Franklin; the Estate of Joseph Gallo; Myron Sugerman and the Estate of Barney Sugerman Z'l ; Thomas Masseria and the Estate of Guissepe Masseria; the Estate of Salvatore Luciano; the Estate of Jimmy Alo; the Estate of Samuel Margolis; Thomas, Ginger, and Havana Selleck; and Mr. Frank, Mike, Bobby, and the ghosts of President Street who took me for a *walk*—down memory lane.

Introduction

It would be difficult, if not fundamentally impossible, for contemporary historians to overestimate the degree of influence that organized crime has exerted upon the development of New York City as a global metropolis, and the opposite can be said to hold true as well. "If I can make it there, I'll make it anywhere"—or so an iconic song line endorses—and countless upstart pioneers of New York's criminal underworld who began operating in the city that never sleeps after the start of National Prohibition may as well have penned that venerated lyric themselves.

The United States of America was perceived by 19th-century intellectuals like Ralph Waldo Emerson as a "smelting pot" for tens of millions of eastern European immigrants, and it was inarguably New York City that provided our fledgling nation's largest single concentration of human ore. Yet deep therein, as organic as it was unpredictable, were some of mankind's most potent impurities: mad micks, Cosa Nostra capos, and Yiddish-tongued no-goodniks. There, amid the legitimate refugees and castaways intent on a new life abroad, huddled those who had been shooed away from the lands of their births and were inadvertently turned loose on a society they adopted, if not by choice, then out of need for a place to hang their hats. It was, among other factors, this very abrupt integration of diverse nationalities within the relatively small but densely inhabited geographical areas of Manhattan, Brooklyn, Queens, the Bronx, and Staten Island that sparked and sustained decades of brutal power struggles, at last developing into gangland's often conspicuous domination over New York City's lucrative lifebloods: construction, transportation, entertainment, garments, sanitation, and vice.

New York City's extraordinary concentrations of wealth represented unbounded possibilities to the early shapers of organized crime, most perceptibly men like Salvatore Luciana, whose Americanized alias—Charles "Lucky" Luciano—can be found permanently ranked amid *Time* magazine's "Heroes and Icons of the 20th Century," ceremonially inducted alongside masters of industry or invention like Henry Ford and Bill Gates. His beginnings were somewhat less auspicious, however, and in 1906, Luciano disembarked at Ellis Island cloaked in poverty like virtually all of his compatriots. Unlike the ungovernable criminal Neanderthals who paved the way toward Luciano's ultimate grab for supremacy, though, the vision of "gangsterdom" that Luciano promoted was as orderly as a map of Manhattan; or, perhaps more exactly, as a branch of Chase-Manhattan.

Under Luciano's tutelage, New York City's most discordant and predatory elements would for the first time possess a complex inner structure and become as fiscally solvent as the soundest U.S. corporation—sounder, in actual fact, throughout the depths of the Great Depression when modern racketeering's grand blueprint was first implemented. Discarding a business model whose equivalent was thumping innocent bystanders over the head and rifling their wallets—as so many of Luciano's heavy-handed predecessors betrayed their preference for—organized crime's new deal was considerably more innovative, and when the 18th Amendment fell to repeal in 1933, the criminal ranks Luciano marshaled would put away their whiskey stills and commence siphoning profits from the rest of Gotham's most vital industries, all the while tacitly acknowledging a crucial economic reality: that it was more advantageous to dominate a small percentage of something than the lion's share of nothing. Above all, though, organized crime's bold restructuring relied upon a hierarchy of authority to be obeyed in all matters pertaining to the fleecing of New York City, its taxpayers, consumers, and environs.

For the first half of the 20th century and beyond, the City of New York and its residents were relatively easy pickings for organized crime's founding godfathers and virtually no better proving ground existed for an up and coming swindle. The city's bulging sea ports were powerful magnets for precious cargo from around the globe and yet they were seemingly defenseless against hijackers; its marketplaces were driven by capitalist spirit and corruption in equally fervent parts; its mayor's office and court systems were called "Tin Box Parades," vulnerable to extortion and solicitous of bribery; and its sidewalks were populated by ordinary citizens inclined to patronize the underworld's thriving black market—both to seize an edge over their own business competitors and to simply make their private lives more inhabitable in times of deep financial adversity. It was within this cacophonous environment, largely, that organized crime in New York City would put down roots, mature, and flourish.

It should come as no surprise that New York City, perhaps to a greater degree than any other urban center, has contributed to the rampant cross-pollination of organized crime throughout the United States. From Alphonse Capone's blood-bathed ascendancy in Chicagoland to Benjamin "Bugsy" Siegel's desert dream—fabulous Las Vegas, Nevada—an overwhelming number of the American mob's most felonious carpetbaggers could trace their roots to the place where they had first honed their particular talents: the five boroughs.

Most of the criminal personalities who established New York's "Mob Scene" are gone now except within the pages of books such as this one, but as more than a handful of these seldom-circulated images can attest, the visual appeal of the Big Apple as a backdrop for organized crime in its most critical period does, in fact, still resonate loudly to this day. Many of the back alleys and haunts that lent their air and aura to the folklore of gangland still stand intact and again—to a more significant extent than anywhere else in the nation—are readily available to contemporary inner-city adventurers.

More significantly, perhaps, New York City persists as the smelting pot of alien émigrés that Emerson described two centuries ago and, as if by some official charter, it remains a nurturing environment for organized crime's newest-emerging rackets—the books and movies about which have yet to be written. Endowed with scores of teeming industries and a certain ease with which one can float anonymously—invisibly, even—between diverse social circles, gangland's enduring presence here may well be attributable to many of the same comforts its law-abiding citizens find irresistible.

One

Rags to Riches

Lessons of Prohibition

Yielding to the demands of a long-suffering Temperance Movement and its dogged Anti-Saloon League lobbyists, the U.S. Congress officially ratified a policy of National Prohibition in 1919 that criminalized the distillation, import, distribution, and sale of alcoholic beverages not expressly approved for medicinal consumption. A dry martini in a New York City barroom after January 16, 1920, no longer required vermouth. In fact, it meant no inebriates at all—and for a period lasting 13 years.

Commonly referred to as the "Noble Experiment" and so-called by then president Herbert Hoover, a similar strain of social experimentation had been attempted in the past, albeit with little success; the adoption of the Harrison Tax Act of 1915, for instance, forbade the unregulated dispensation of narcotics by doctors and pharmacists, encouraging underworld elements to introduce heroin, cocaine, and morphine onto their black market—converting the drug addicted into avid consumers. It was a demographic that included such improbable clientele as housewives throughout the Midwest, and racketeers could not ignore this opportunity to expand their presence beyond New York City's regional boundaries.

The Volstead Law, as the National Prohibition Act was also known, proved itself virtually impossible for New York City's police agencies to enforce and became immediately unfashionable with urbanites whose liberal ways of thinking in the self-styled Jazz Age did not necessarily align themselves with the Anti-Saloon League's own, nor with the organization's poorly camouflaged underpinnings of religious idealism. In fact, many city dwellers considered the nation's "dry" laws to be a frontal assault upon personal freedoms guaranteed to them by the Bill of Rights. Although the movement was initially conceived as a cure-all for society's criminal ills, forced abstinence from alcohol would accomplish the exact opposite objective by amplifying New York City's crime rates exponentially and making spectacularly rich men of daring but predictable bootleggers who then parlayed their rapidly gaining material wealth into political influence—all while stealthily hidden behind the scenes.

In this previously unpublished image dated December 19, 1919, an 18-year-old Arthur Flegenheimer—yet to be rechristened "Dutch Schultz"—is portrayed at the start of his first and only incarceration. The future "Beer Baron of the Bronx" was paroled the very next year by a prison warden named *Brew*ster, oddly enough, and Flegenheimer would hurriedly become the most vindictive and

feared bootlegger of the Prohibition era. Grossly undereducated and a moving target for both law enforcement and fellow gangsters alike, Schultz nevertheless enjoyed a longer, more profitable reign than many of his contemporaries. (Author's collection.)

This is the earliest known portrait of Arnold Rothstein, New York City gambler and mentor to a generation of racketeering figures who, according to testimony, schemed to rig the 1919 World Series in his favor—staining the national pastime's reputation for decades. In an era before digital airbrushing, this snapshot underwent certain changes from the original; most notably, Rothstein was sporting a casual straw boater's hat the morning he encountered paparazzi in Manhattan, but instead a sinister-looking grey fedora was skillfully painted atop his head by an anonymous news editor keen to make a bold impression on his readership. (Author's collection.)

George "Hump" McManus, author of this far-from-exculpatory letter, was tried and acquitted of Arnold Rothstein's murder, and if there were eyewitnesses to the gunplay at Manhattan's Park Central Hotel in November 1928, none came forward to say who shot the renowned racketeer, then sent the murder weapon sailing out a third-floor window to the street. Rothstein would also decline to name his killer during a speakeasy séance the next year, but while among the living, he tutored a generation of budding mobsters like Salvatore "Lucky" Luciano, Meyer Lansky, and even slovenly Arthur "Dutch Schultz" Flegenheimer to comport themselves as if skirting the law was, in fact, a legitimate business pursuit. Practicing what he preached, Rothstein's mortgage company (below) collateralizes the corporate stock of a Manhattan cosmetics supplier to whom he loaned money to stay afloat. (Right, Avi Bash collection; below, author's collection.)

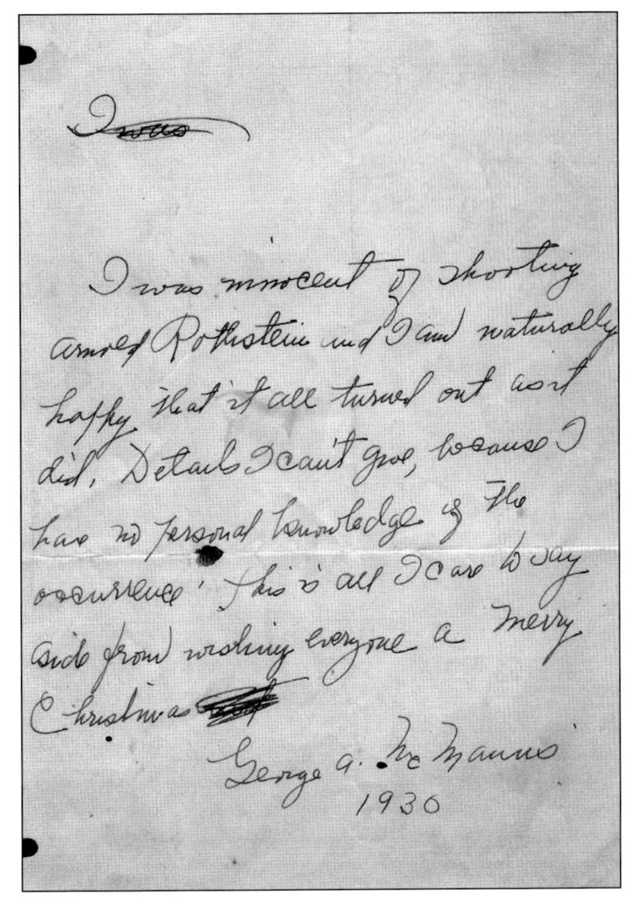

I was innocent of shooting Arnold Rothstein and I am naturally happy that it all turned out as it did, Details I can't give, because I have no personal knowledge of the occurrence. This is all I care to say aside from wishing everyone a Merry Christmas

George A. McManus
1930

December 24th, 1926

We hereby acknowledge receipt of the following certificate of stock of Adolph Klar Inc., which are to be held by us as collateral for a loan in accordance with the terms entered into between Adolph Klar and the Rothmere Mortgage Corporation, made on the 23rd day of November 1926.

Certificate #1	- 10 shares of	common capital stock.	
"	6 - 40 shares of	Preferred capital stock.	
"	7 - 50 shares of	"	" "
"	8 - 50 shares of	"	" "
"	9 - 50 shares of	"	" "
"	10 - 50 shares of	"	" "
"	11 - 50 shares of	"	" "
"	12 - 50 shares of	"	" "
"	13 - 50 shares of	"	" "
"	14 - 50 shares of	"	" "

Also Assignment Marvin W. Clarke to Adolph Klar
" Adolph Klar to Adolph Klar, Inc.

ROTHMERE MORTGAGE CORPORATION

The last of the so-called "Mustache Pete" mafia who rejected the thought of fraternizing except with old-world Italians, it was Guissepe "Joe the Boss" Masseria's characteristic resistance to change that placed him squarely in harm's way, and ultimately, Masseria's iron-fisted control over New York City's bootlegging marketplace would be taken by force, along with his life, by the hired guns he trusted most. Here Masseria is seen in a private family moment with his wife and his namesake, Joe Jr., one of nine adult sons. (Masseria family collection.)

On holiday with his wife around March 1930, bootlegger Guiseppe "Joe the Boss" Masseria bridged an evolutionary gap between "Black Hand" mafia extortionists and a more innovative generation of racketeers represented by Salvatore "Lucky" Luciano, Masseria's own lieutenant, who accompanied him on this Floridian vacation. They were among 19 arrested for patronizing an illegal gambling hall that police said occupied an entire floor of their Miami resort hotel. Meanwhile, at home in Manhattan, heavyweights of the Little Italy "Whiskey Curb" (right) kept friends close but enemies closer while pursuing bootleg liquor profits—literally surrounding police headquarters with a roving black market that operated each weekend until late 1922 when, a block away, Masseria fired 60 shots at rival Rocco Valenti but instead hit a half-dozen innocent bystanders. (Above, Masseria family collection; right, author's collection.)

He would have entered history as "Snorkey" instead of "Scarface" if not for his upbringing as a New York City street tough and an encounter with the blade of a Brooklyn thug in a barroom on Coney Island's bowery. Alphonse Capone (in a classic Jantzen swimsuit) exported his criminal acumen to Chicago in time for the start of Prohibition, causing greater carnage there than any other gangland practitioner. Among Capone's mentors back home was Guissepe "Joe the Boss" Masseria, with whom he maintained a close intercity alliance, even counseling Masseria that the full might of the underworld was mounting against him. In this image, preserved by relatives of Capone in Naples, Italy, the gang boss cradles a nephew, Ralph "Risky" Capone. (Author's collection.)

Appearing businesslike in every detail, this is the formal portrait of himself that Salvatore "Lucky" Luciano selected for presentation to his friends and family. During his youth in the streets of New York City's destitute lower east side, Luciano had ample opportunity to observe the rise of men such as Richard Croker, the one-time leader of the "4th Avenue Tunnel Gang" who traded his brass knuckles for a seat at the political table. As such, Croker excelled in thievery but on a relatively small scale, whereas Luciano's own version of criminality mimicked the corporate America of capitalist giants J. P. Morgan and John D. Rockefeller. Luciano also recognized a greater benefit in subverting public officials than in seeking elected office himself. (Author's collection.)

A World War I surplus machine gun sits mounted on the bow of this harbor police steamer, seen dry-docked near City Island during the onset of National Prohibition. Open-water pursuits and automatic gunfire were common in the hunt for bootleggers, whose intoxicating cargo supplied the city's rumored 30,000 speakeasies. When the U.S. Coast Guard reported in 1925 that smugglers were acquiring lightning-quick speedboats, no amount of retooling could save the sluggish steamer. The last of these dinosaurs was mothballed the very next year in favor of a fully gasoline-powered fleet. (Both, author's collection.)

Richard E. Enright filled the post of police commissioner throughout the "Bootleg Wars," in the early 1920s. Though accused of accepting graft from the same warring bootleggers, Enright brought charges against his own men who failed to enforce the Volstead Act and established 24-hour vice patrols to harass gambling houses. He resigned in 1925 to become a crime writer, finding prose simpler to manipulate than the flow of illegal liquor. (Author's collection.)

In this image purged from the files of the New York Police Department, an unidentified victim of Prohibition violence lays dead amid a cache of loaded shotguns and half-filled wine glasses. He, not unlike countless others, learned with terrifying finality that in Gotham's criminal underworld, no one was getting ahead armed merely with a "Please" and "Thank you." (Author's collection.)

Photographed by Brooklyn's Ferrantino Studios, Joseph Bonanno began his rise to mafia prominence as a top strategist for Salvatore Maranzano, chief rival of Guissepe "Joe the Boss" Masseria—both of whom would fall victim to a Salvatore "Lucky" Luciano double-cross. Bonanno's invasion of Masseria's bootlegging territories on behalf of Maranzano's faction ignited the Castellammarese War, and with Maranzano's assassination in late 1931, Bonanno astutely aligned himself with Luciano. By doing so, Bonanno inherited most of the slain man's rackets and all the extravagance their spoils afforded him. (Author's collection.)

Dominating city politics throughout the 1920s was the Democratic Party, whose headquarters occupied a high-pillared fortress nicknamed Tammany Hall (above), near Union Square. Though excoriated for permissiveness toward gangsters, Tammany had little competition. As the second Tammany-endorsed mayor during Prohibition, James "Jimmy" Walker (below) had nicknames also, surprisingly few of which were pejorative. Walker was intensely admired while he shunned moralistic bylaws, attended speakeasies, divorced his devoted albeit frumpy wife to wed a flapper girl, christened Riker's Island Prison but did little to populate it, and resigned during a corruption inquiry. An office aide took this snapshot of dandified hizzoner "Beau James" in 1929. On its verso, it states Walker is "reading the many telegrams congratulating him on his re-election for Mayor of the City of New York over LaGuardia by record Plurality of 497,165." (Both, author's collection.)

In this remarkable Prohibition-era image, the New York City Police Department's motorcycle brigade parades its latest arsenal in the uniformly uphill battle against purveyors of illegal liquor. There was no more appropriate a venue for unveiling the speedy fleet of Indian Chiefs—capable of outrunning the fastest bootlegger's sedan—than along the former "Whiskey Curb" directly outside NYPD headquarters. (Author's collection.)

A closer examination of the same image reveals that among the spectators eyeballing the new machinery that day—and inadvertently caught by the department's official photographer—were several of New York City's most conspicuous bad men, including (starting fourth from left) Benjamin "Bugsy" Siegel, Meyer Lansky, Vincent "Jimmy Blue Eyes" Alo, and his close friend, waterfront gangster Eddie McGrath. (Author's collection.)

Arrested by the NYPD in January 1933 were, from left to right, Guido Pati, Battisto Salvo, Frank Alo, and Frank Sgambati. Alo, the brother of Vincent "Jimmy Blue Eyes" Alo, was identified by the Bronx district attorney as the "Syndicate's representative" for loan-sharking, charging unconscionable rates of interest and doling out beatings to those who failed to pay. Associates of Arthur "Dutch Schultz" Flegenheimer later kidnapped Battisto Salvo. Within one week of his release, four of Salvo's kidnappers were killed, a fifth committed suicide, and another was left for dead beside Manhattan's Metropolitan Museum of Art. (Author's collection.)

E. R. MOSHER CO. INC.
PULP AND PAPER
51 EAST 42ND ST.
NEW YORK CITY Monday -

November 20th, 1922.

Dear Mr. Chipman;

The enclosed should be able to give you a thrill.

Paper business is pretty rotten - so am trying to make an "Honest" living this way.

If you can use anything on the enclosed list don't fail to let me know.

Would very much like to buy you a good lunch when your not too busy, and hope this finds you in the best.

Saw the plant recently - and have got to hand it to you. Sure looks like a million dollars.

Best regards,
M. Deverich

His surname rhymed with "beverage" and this letter from Manhattan paper manufacturer Maurice Deverich required little guessing as to the source of his income during Prohibition. His "list" offered 23 whiskies, 10 champagnes, gin, rum, absinthe, and Canadian ale boasting 7.5-percent alcohol. To appear legitimate, Deverich bought paper on credit then sold it at a loss—a practice that invited police attention whereas selling bootleg liquor never did. (Author's collection.)

Phile Aquilino (in a monogrammed swimsuit) and his brother Frank adopted the alias "Ross," which they also named their trucking company on Mulberry Street in Manhattan, which was first used to supply huge quantities of brown sugar to untaxed whiskey distilleries both during and after Prohibition. Aquilino is seen on holiday with underworld associates identified as his cousin "Mikey Ross" (far left) and "Frankie Bananas," a reputed "running board gunman" for the Charles Luciano mob. When Luciano underboss Vito Genovese and his aide Peter DeFeo were each indicted for the murder of hoodlum Ferdinand "The Shadow" Boccia, Genovese fled to Italy, but DeFeo hid from police at this comfortable resort hotel in Tennanah Lake, New York. (Aquilino family collection.)

DO YOU WANT TO–

PUT THE CRIMINAL OUT OF BUSINESS?

HELP THE UNEMPLOYED?

National Prohibition is the Law which makes it possible for the Criminal Class to Roll Up Huge Fortunes while Honest Citizens walk the streets in search of jobs.

Millions of Dollars are now Wasted on Futile Attempts at Enforcement when Every Dollar is needed to Aid the Unemployed.

JOIN THE

Women's Organization For National Prohibition Reform

WORK AND VOTE FOR REPEAL OF THE 18TH AMENDMENT!

Just the variety of bootlegger this anti-Prohibition broadside (above) railed against, David Berman (below) was also a renowned bank thief and gambling pioneer whose family, like those of Meyer Lansky and Benjamin "Bugsy" Siegel, immigrated to the United States from Russia. "Davie the Jew" spent his formative years in the American Midwest but made inroads with East Coast crime outfits before appearing on the NYPD's radar in 1927 as part of a gang that abducted a wealthy Brooklyn real estate tycoon and another man who was one-half of a liquor smuggling ring. (Above, author's collection; below, Avi Bash collection.)

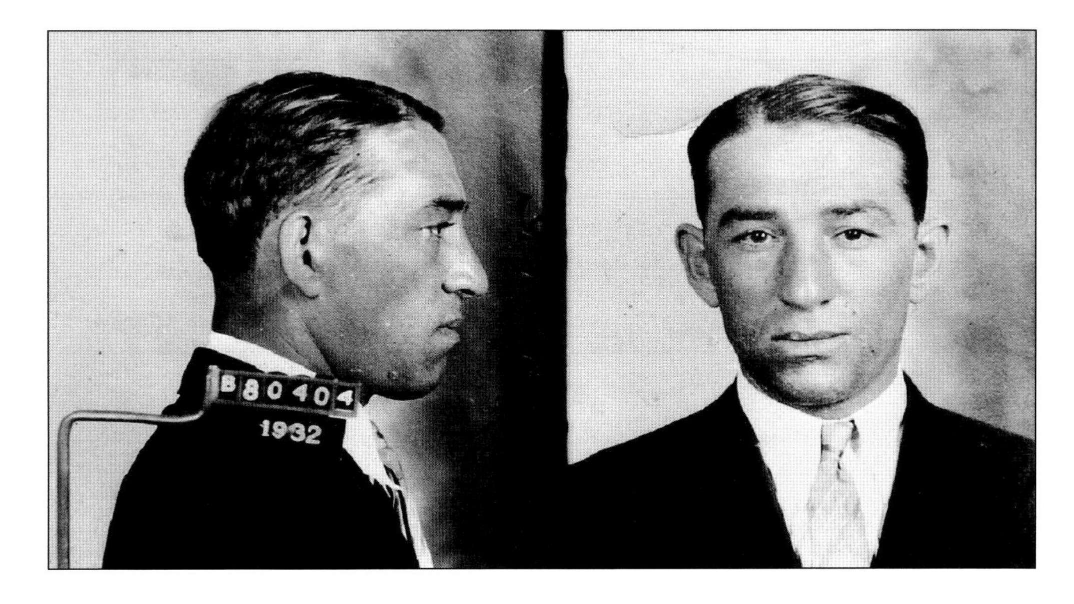

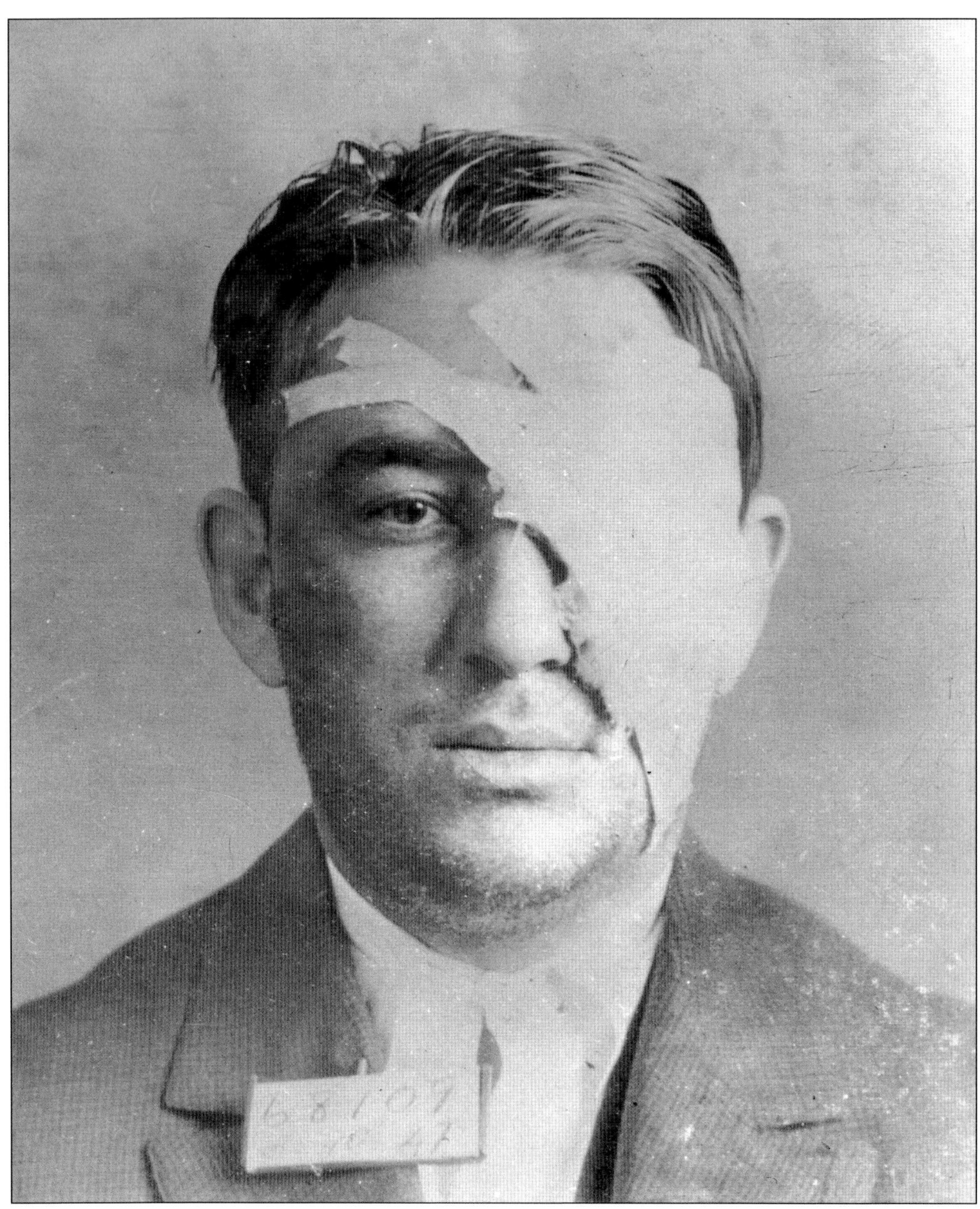

Detective John Cordes tailed David Berman and a second suspect across Manhattan, observing one man hit 29 of 30 bull's-eyes at a Times Square shooting gallery before confronting them on a West Sixty-Sixth Street stoop. Cordes seized Berman's own revolver and swung it hard against the gangster's skull, opening a gash. When the second man reached for a pistol, he was instantly shot dead by motorcycle patrolman Richard O'Connor. The *New York Times* reported Berman was "a huge man, of very rough appearance and either he or his accomplice, apparently, could have killed Detective Cordes with ease in a physical encounter." Unmoved by interrogation, Berman remarked, "The worst I can get is life;" but even that was not to be when the kidnapped men could not identify him. (Author's collection.)

Among the stunning episodes of the Castellammarese War was the killing of Guissepe "Joe the Boss" Masseria, which occurred here inside the former Villa Tammaro, a Coney Island restaurant owned by Gerardo Scarpato, who, at the time of Masseria's death, was himself extorting money from a small businessman he summoned to this location on April 15, 1931. "As soon as I reached the place," wrote the frightened entrepreneur to the Brooklyn district attorney, "Scarpato ran over to my car and asked me what I was doing there. Scarpato told me to leave right away and not mention to anyone I had been there that day. I left. Late that night I read that Joe Masseria had been killed at the Villa Tammaro. This was my first taste of what these men were capable of." (City of New York.)

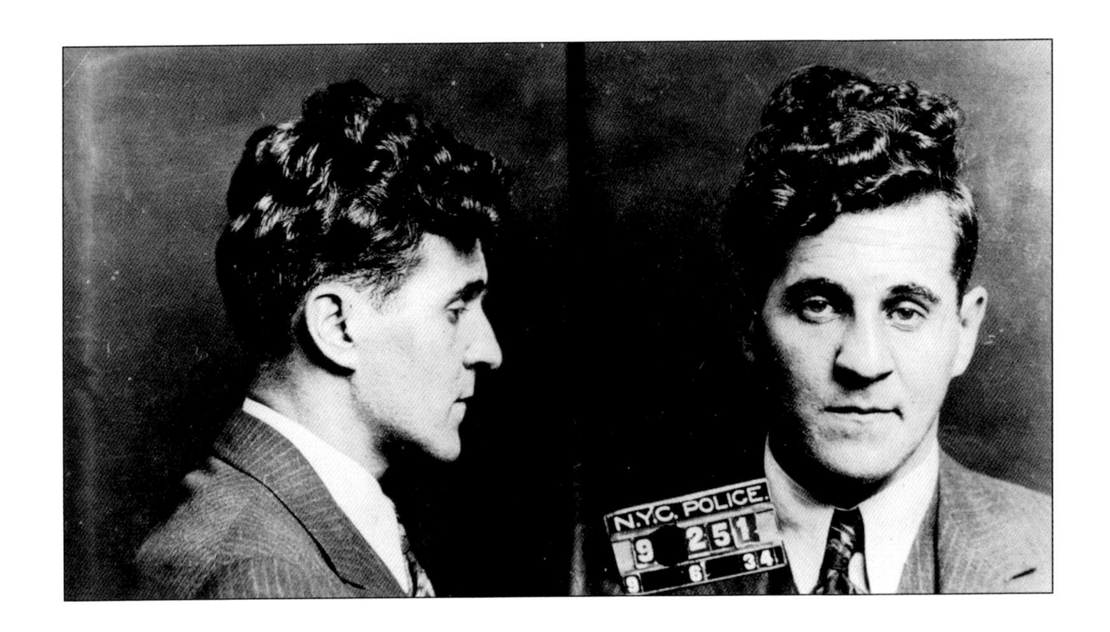

One of the New York City Police Department's finest apprehensions occurred in the final months of Prohibition when eagle-eyed Brooklyn detective Philip Wagg—enjoying a week's vacation with his family at a resort hotel in Monticello, New York—inadvertently spotted fugitive gang leader Max Ludkowitz (above), who, along with older brother Meyer "Little Larney" Ludkowitz (below), was being sought by the Kings County Homicide Court for the May 1931 shooting death of bootlegger Morris Fishbein. For three months, the Ludkowitz brothers were hiding in plain sight, operating a speakeasy, which Detective Wagg's reinforcements from Brooklyn promptly raided to discover both men unarmed, with Max behind the bar serving drinks. In spite of Wagg's exceptional police work, no witnesses to Fishbein's murder came forward and neither Ludkowitz brother was held accountable. (Both, author's collection.)

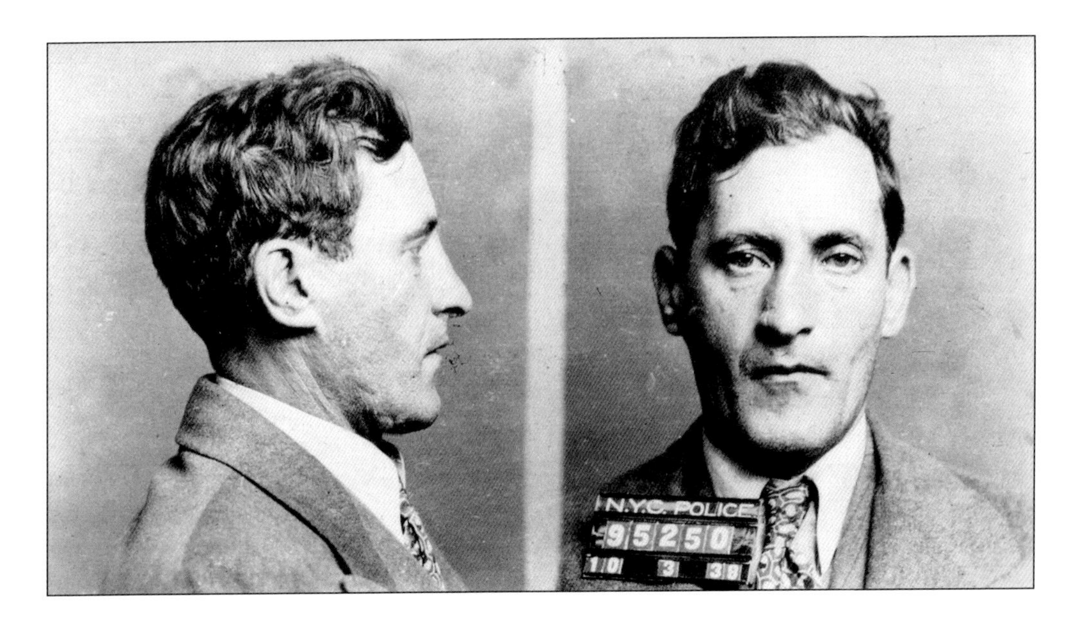

Two

Blood on Velvet

Making Crime Pay

Paraded in a one-man lineup for the benefit of 200 police officials, a boyish-faced murder suspect from Brooklyn named Harry "Pep" Strauss seemed unusually relaxed, standing clad in a hand-tailored Chesterfield coat, framed by its plush velveteen collar. Draped beneath it, his ocean-blue suit, crisp shirt, and matching tie were favorably critiqued by a *New York Times* reporter in the audience that afternoon as having been pressed "to razor sharpness" and his brand new grey fedora hat was worn "canted over one eye at a jaunty angle."

Strauss would never actually stand trial for the senseless killing of gas station attendant Alvin Sydnor—only the fourth of many homicide raps that the 25-year-old gun for hire would beat—but New York City's top cop and master of ceremonies, Police Commissioner Lewis J. Valentine, was ready to propose a solution for dealing with underworld executioners such as this.

"When you meet men like Harry Strauss, don't be afraid to muss 'em up!" boomed Valentine to the appreciative crowd of New York City's finest that packed the room. "Men like him should be mussed up! Blood should be smeared all over his velvet collar. Instead, he looks as though he just came out of the barber shop."

Although the district attorney of Brooklyn responded with a statement flatly condemning police brutality in the pursuit of crime syndicates, Commissioner Valentine continued to speak on behalf of an expanding majority within New York City law enforcement who had grown uncomfortable with the corruption and graft that discredited their profession under previous administrations and who were embarrassed by colleagues that quietly tolerated organized crime as it gained an ever firmer grip on the city's economy. But in spite of the Kings County chief prosecutor's comments, the sentiments of police officers under Lewis Valentine's direction were unwavering, and so was their commissioner:

"Make it disagreeable for these men," Valentine recommended to his small but dedicated militia of boys in blue. "Drive them out of the city. Make them fear arrest. Make them fear *you*. Make them learn that this town is no place for muscle men or racketeers!"

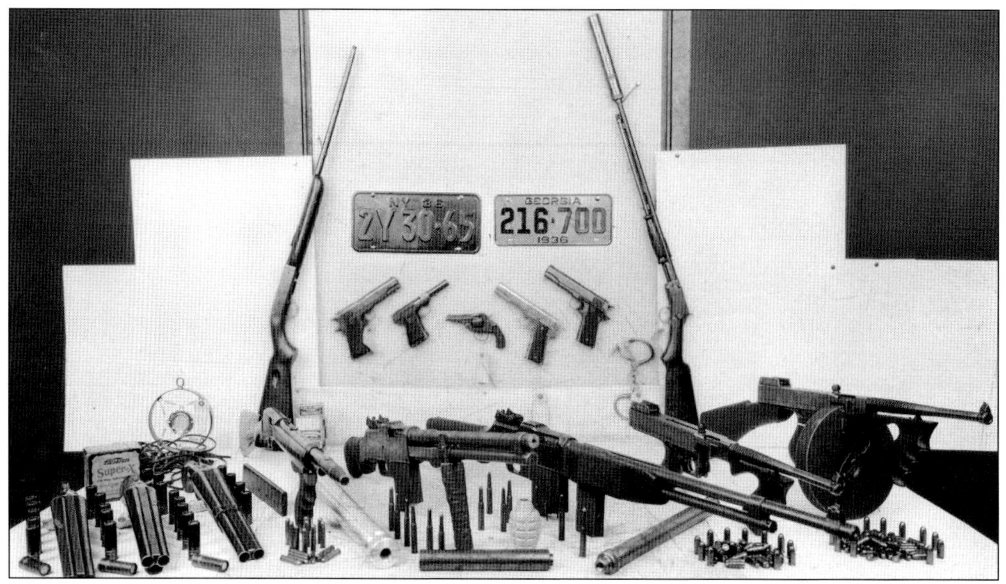

NYPD detectives predicted an epic gunfight before storming the Manhattan hideout of what their police commissioner called "a desperate Mob" in March 1936, but instead they interrupted a ham and egg breakfast. A steel safe in a third floor closet hid the implements of warfare, including Thompson submachine guns, a Browning automatic rifle, sawed-off shotguns, one grenade, and 10,000 rounds of ammunition—earning them a nickname: "The Arsenal Gang." (Author's collection.)

Mayor Fiorello H. LaGuardia (far left), Lewis J. Valentine (second from right), and district attorneys of three boroughs pose during the ritual sinking of pistols, rifles, and slot machines impounded during their revitalized assault on organized crime. "The punks who owned these guns are up the river now," LaGuardia said of 5,000 weapons disposed of in the briny Long Island Sound. "Let's keep up the good work," the mayor encouraged, "and make New York a better place to live in." (Author's collection.)

"Here you see a splendid display of police energy," boasted Mayor LaGuardia, waving a seized firearm for dramatic effect. "The Police Department, with the cooperation of the five District Attorneys, has been able to put the fear of the Lord into the gangsters. Let this be a notice to them that they will be treated just as roughly as we are going to treat these implements." Mayor LaGuardia then swiveled around and put his resolve on display by pitching the sawed-off shotgun into a choppy section of the Long Island Sound. "If anybody can get them back," Police Commissioner Valentine challenged in jest as he discarded a carbine rifle, "they are welcome to them." (Both, author's collection.)

Mayor LaGuardia declared that illegal slot machines in particular, which Commissioner Valentine preferred to call "Mechanical Pickpockets," would be disposed of in the deepest possible waters of the Sound after components of machines confiscated in New York City were later found recycled in gambling devices seized in neighboring New Jersey. Ostensibly, the disassembled parts had been sold as scrap metal but may also have been channeled back to racketeers by corrupt city employees. Here a lonely Mills "Jackpot" machine prepares to meet its everlasting reward along the bottom of the strait. In 1941, LaGuardia expanded his prohibition to include common pinball machines, which he believed corrupted his city's youth. (Both, author's collection.)

"These machines were controlled by the most vicious kind of criminal element," Mayor LaGuardia said as a prelude to the ceremonial mass jettison of contraband that promptly became an annual tradition. LaGuardia told a captive audience how he labored to pass a bill in Congress forbidding the transport of gambling devices across state lines, but that political protection afforded the gangsters who owned the machines had prevented it. "Now," LaGuardia declared, "I've got this thing cleaned up. This racket is now destroyed." The *New York Times* reported that the mayor then swung a sledgehammer "lustily" at a slot machine and sent brass tokens clinking across the deck before turning the task over to Manhattan district attorney William Copeland Dodge and members of his committee. (Both, author's collection.)

As ferry passengers motor past the mayor's flotilla, Police Commissioner Valentine and William Copeland Dodge (above, far left) pose with a bushel of gun barrels destined for the sea floor, each tagged with the identity of a criminal defendant and the case in which they stood convicted. Despite the three-term LaGuardia administration's obvious enthusiasm, its detractors frequently accused it of leaving the business of fighting organized crime to the office of the governor. Dodge would serve just one term as district attorney of Manhattan during which he refused to appoint a special rackets prosecutor, and during the 1937 corruption trial of Tammany Hall politician James "Jimmy" Hines, Dodge was said to have accepted 1933 election funds from bootlegger Arthur "Dutch Schultz" Flegenheimer. (Both, author's collection.)

At the stern end of a city tugboat believed to be nearing Execution Light, approximately 3 miles east of City Island, Queens, Lewis J. Valentine enlists help from official invitees as he heaves overboard the hollowed-out shell of a coin-operated crane amusement along with a half-dozen of several hundred slot machines, as Harbor Patrol officers observe the heavy lifting from a safe distance. To facilitate hoisting the cumbersome devices, many of which were owned by mobster Frank Costello, the commissioner had their innards gutted beforehand at an NYPD warehouse in Brooklyn. (Both, author's collection.)

"Tin-Horn Gangsters" was only one example of creative invective that crime-busting Mayor Fiorello LaGuardia cast at the former owners of these nickel and steel-clad pistols which, in most cases, had violated a New York gun control statute that criminalized the possession of unregistered weapons of any kind. When it was discovered that virtually all of the firearms had been purchased in neighboring states, Commissioner Valentine (examining revolvers, above and below) began promoting the need for a "Federal Sullivan Law" to further thwart their access to the five boroughs. (Both, author's collection.)

Before propelling them over the side, Police Commissioner Valentine played to the cameras and held each weapon aloft to explain its function, including what appears to be a Browning machine gun (above) immobilized by the flame of an acetylene torch. Joined by a revolving cast of Panama-hatted city executives, Valentine was a dedicated participant in most if not all of Mayor LaGuardia's maritime photo ops. One such voyage to a dumping ground off the coast of Connecticut required a nine-hour return trip, and the annual expedition was commonly made in spite of less than favorable seafaring conditions. (Both, author's collection.)

Gov. Herbert H. Lehman probed a Brooklyn murder racket consisting chiefly of fellow Jews and pursued the long-term imprisonment of key racketeers like Salvatore "Lucky" Luciano. Lehman was also a partner in collapsed investment giant Lehman Brothers, thought to be among the corporate models Luciano emulated when restructuring organized crime. This portrait was gifted to the Jewish Anti-Defamation League's Seymour Graubard in Monticello where Lehman and his brand new crime committee probed New York City gangsters frequenting the Catskill Mountains community. (Author's collection.)

Thomas E. Dewey was not Herbert H. Lehman's first, second, or even fourth choice as special prosecutor of Rackets, but he got the nod after all of the governor's initial appointees politely declined. Dewey nevertheless seized his opportunity to rout underworld triggermen like those in the next chapter, as well as corrupt public officials who permitted themselves to fall under gangland influence. He continued the trend as Manhattan district attorney. (Author's collection.)

Al Marinelli, the powerful Tammany Hall district leader who associated openly with Salvatore "Lucky" Luciano, became a primary target for Rackets prosecutor Thomas E. Dewey. Marinelli agreed to provide political protection for narcotics distributorships (as seen above, captured by the NYPD), as well as for Luciano's loan-sharking to Manhattan prostitutes at cutthroat rates of interest. Among those reined in by Dewey, Russian-born bookmaker Benjamin "Benny" Spiller was convicted of vice racketeering alongside star defendant Luciano. Before he could be sentenced, Dewey convinced the aptly named Spiller to provide information in exchange for a reduction in his prison term—from 50 years to merely five. (Both, author's collection.)

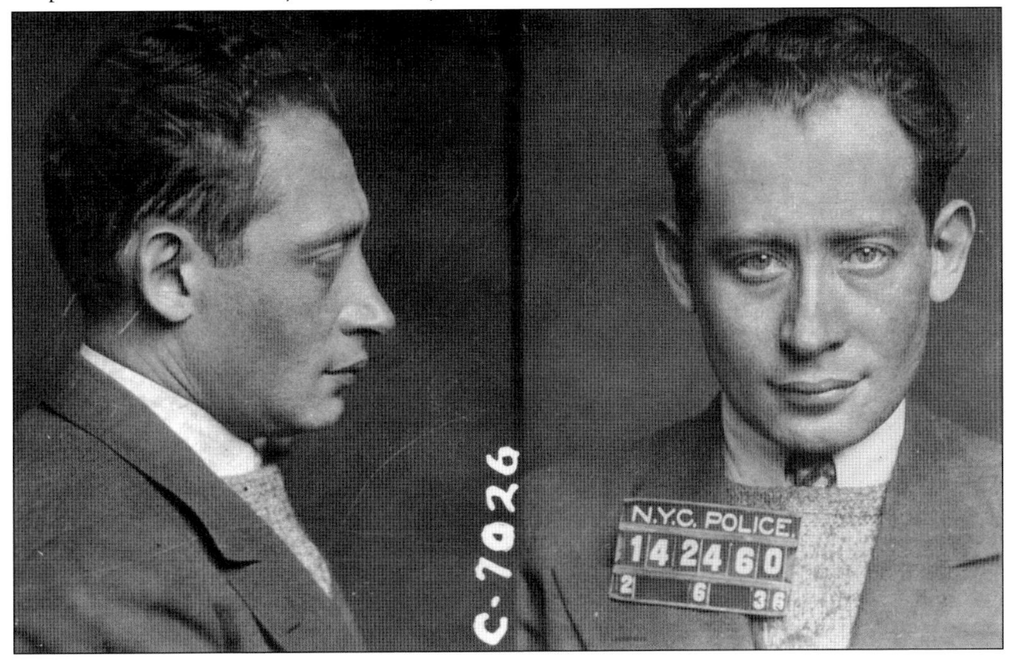

Located by his family amid Salvatore "Lucky" Luciano's private effects at the time of his death was this candid image taken very shortly after his early parole from Sing Sing Prison and permanent expulsion from the United States. Luciano's lady friend is Igea Lissoni, the retired Italian ballerina who became a constant companion during his life in involuntary exile. (Author's collection.)

Salvatore "Lucky" Luciano enjoys the company of American tourist Gertrude Gaskin in Italy, where his movements were restricted and monitored by the government. Barred from reentering the United States, Luciano nevertheless sailed to foreign ports and was involved with the ground-breaking of extravagant casinos in prerevolutionary Cuba, where a greater share of the New York mob's money gravitated once Mayor Fiorello LaGuardia and Thomas E. Dewey upped the ante on underworld gambling. (Avi Bash collection.)

Three

Guns and Gelt
The Kosher Nostra

At virtually the same moment that New York City law enforcement was girding resources to expand its racket-busting capabilities under the anticorruption mayor, Fiorello LaGuardia, and his hard-hitting police commissioner, Lewis J. Valentine, the ruling bodies of organized crime were likewise acknowledging an ever-present need to enforce their own distinct edicts, which increasingly more often required extermination of enemies, associates, and business competitors. Even lifelong friends were not impervious to a gangland fusillade if their death was predicted to profit or otherwise enrich the organization in the future.

The leaders of New York City's major crime factions, headed by former Prohibition bootleggers of varying ethnicities, would realize how impossible it was to nurture an empire while in jail awaiting trial or in hiding from a homicide charge and therefore sought to convince a select group of street hoods from the largely immigrant enclaves of Brownsville and Ocean Hill, Brooklyn, to dedicate themselves to slay-for-pay; in consideration of a healthy monthly stipend, they would restrict their carnage to the fulfillment of specific murder assignments supplied by deep-pocketed superiors such as Manhattan Garment District heavyweight Louis "Lepke" Buchalter and Brooklyn waterfront racketeer Albert Anastasia. The removal of would-be prosecution witnesses became their stock-in-trade.

While significantly less sophisticated than the men for whom they toiled, this predominantly Jewish-populated hit squad was extraordinarily efficient, carrying out potentially hundreds of unanswered murders throughout New York City, along the Eastern Seaboard, and as far west as Los Angeles. In a period that long preceded modern police technology, it was often sufficient that the intended victim was not personally acquainted with his appointed killer for that crime to go permanently unsolved. But no truth being absolute, this hopeful foray into committing the perfect murder suffered from fatal flaws and, in due course, would introduce the concept of "snitching" to the American lexicon.

25
14059

There were fedora hats aplenty but few storybook endings for the paid gunmen of organized crime's enforcement arm, known as "Murder, Inc.," seen here in the custody of the NYPD. Adept killers all, in the end a few saved their own skins by testifying for the Brooklyn district attorney while others went on to die in the electric chair at Sing Sing Prison. From left to right are Martin "Buggsy" Goldstein (booked under the alias "Al Goodman"), Emilio Corrigano, Nathan "Nat" Katzman, Harry "Happy" Maione, Vito "Chickenhead" Gurino, Anthony Varrichio, and Larry Mazzarise. (Author's collection.)

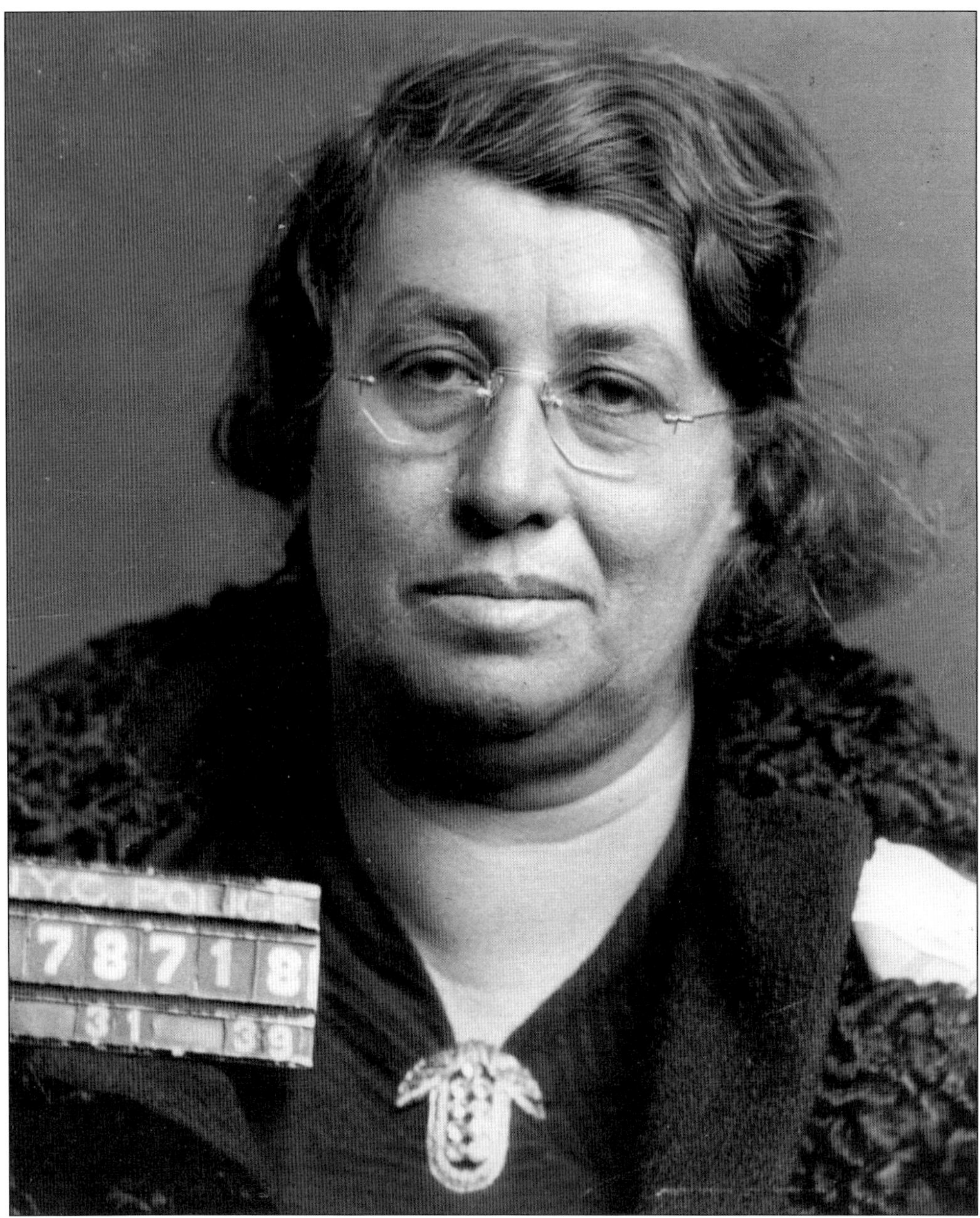

One may not be tempted to think of matriarchal Lena Frosch as the original "Bond Girl," but what Frosch lacked in physical endowments she more than made up for in moxie. Seen here in 1939 under arrest on 24 counts of forgery, it was Frosch and her family-run bail-bond racket that catered to keeping Murder, Inc. heavyweights at liberty to do Louis "Lepke" Buchalter's bidding. Frosch's activities were first exposed during a four-month-long inquiry into official corruption by Brooklyn special prosecutor John Harlan Amen, who later served as chief interrogator during the Nazi trials at Nuremberg. His investigation resulted in Police Commissioner Lewis Valentine's dismissal of nearly one dozen high-ranking officers, each found guilty of accepting fraudulently written bonds. (Author's collection.)

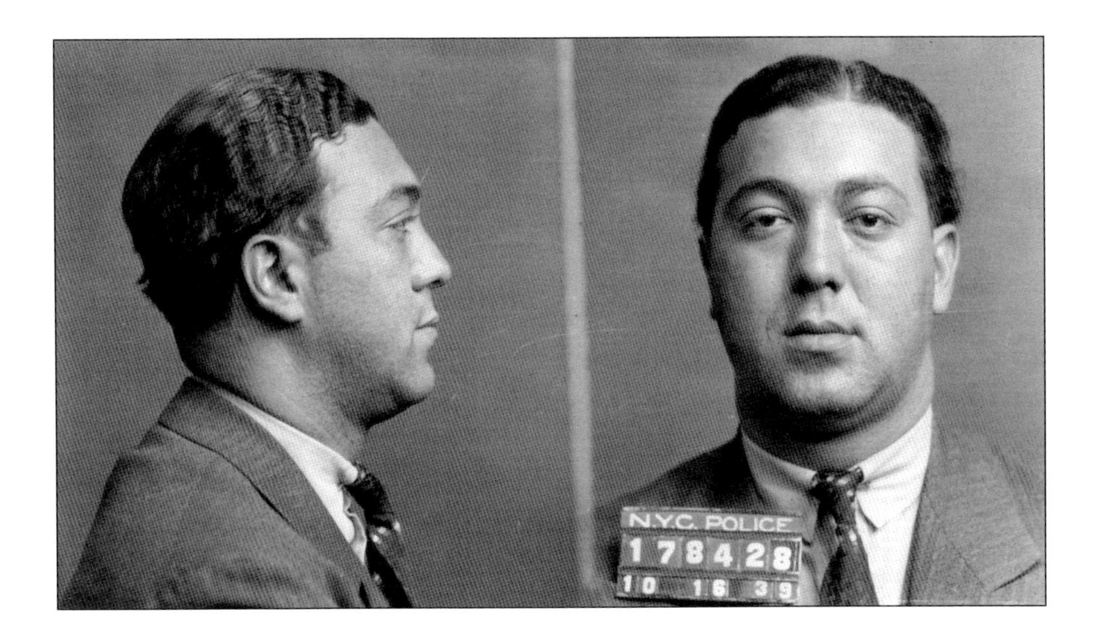

Sporting a finger-wave hairstyle and described by a *New York Times* reporter as dressing "in the latest Broadway styles," Abraham Frosch was a chip off the old block, learning the bail-bond trade during countless childhood visits to police stations with his father, Irving (below). His knowledge of police corruption led him to remark as an informant for prosecutor John Harlan Amen: "I know station houses that can be bought for four dollars." While under Amen's supervision, Frosch was permitted to leave custody to meet with Brownsville gunmen Abe Reles and Martin "Buggsy" Goldstein and conveyed the pair's $5,000 bribe offer to a murder witness who, coincidentally, was housed in the jail cell beside Frosch's. But no provision was made for codefendant Anthony "Duke" Maffatore, who returned the favor by cooperating with the district attorney. (Both, author's collection.)

In partnership with Benjamin "Bugsy" Siegel, freckle-faced gunman Samuel "Red" Levine owned a Brooklyn bail-bond office, too, and participated in the Castellammarese War killings of Guissepe "Joe the Boss" Masseria and his chief bootlegging rival, Salvatore Maranzano, five months later. Jewish hit men like Levine were the chosen people, in a manner of speaking, because it was calculated that the old world Italians they aimed to kill would never see them coming. And although his profile in 1935 did not reveal the presence of a traditional *yarmulke*, Levine was rumored to have had a religious streak which—or so it has been passed into folklore—forbade him from exercising his trigger finger on the Jewish Sabbath. (Author's collection.)

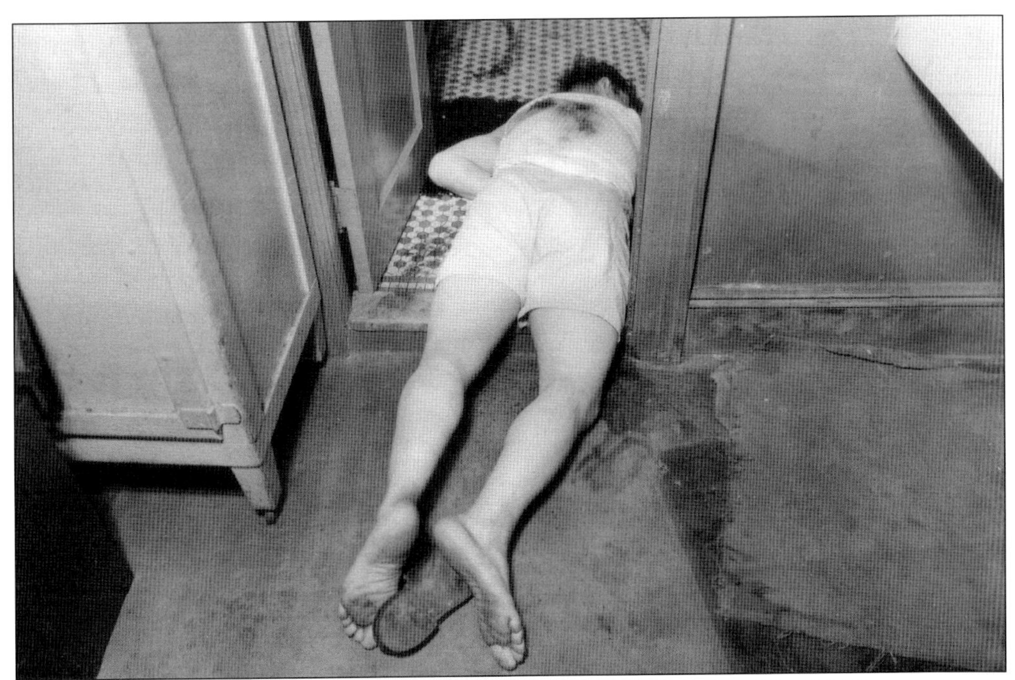

In these long-unidentified images lies one of two slain plasterers named by NYPD investigators as Cesaro Lattaro and Antonio Siciliano, who were killed in their basement apartment on Bergen Street in Brooklyn as a result of a labor racketeering dispute. Also shot down by Vito "Chickenhead" Gurino, Frank "Dasher" Abbandando, and Harry "Happy" Maione, who allegedly dressed in women's clothing during the commission of this double homicide, was the pair's pet bulldog, located by police detectives in the bathroom shower. District attorney William O'Dwyer would describe the perpetrators as "killing for the love of it." (Both, author's collection.)

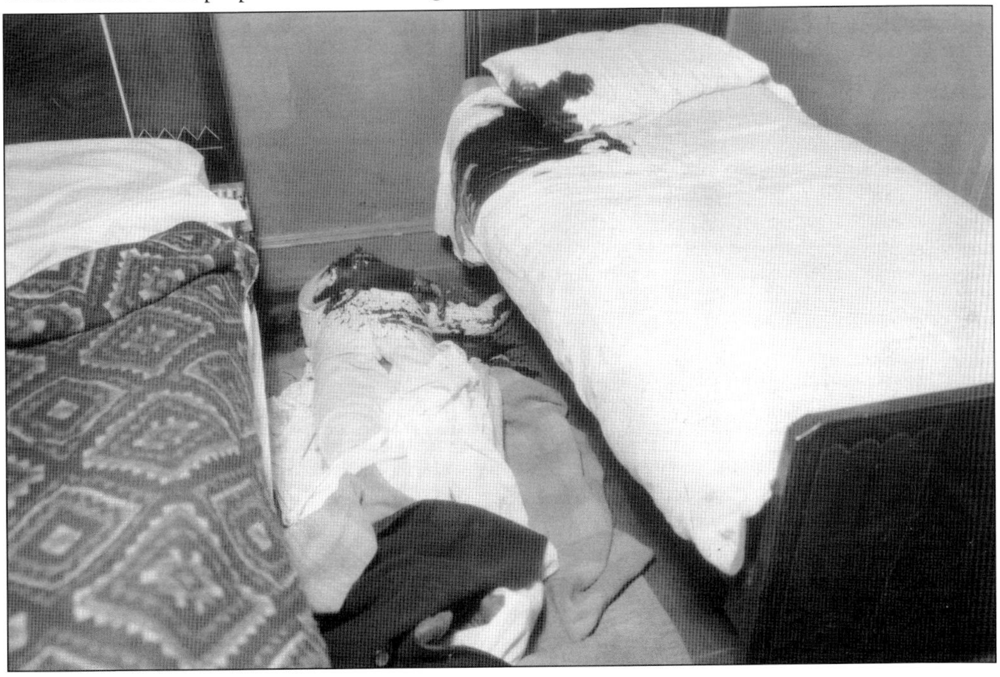

When famously hard-nosed Police Commissioner Lewis Valentine spoke to his uniformed flock of smearing blood on the velvety collars of mobsters, he was pointing a finger at none other than Harry "Pep" Strauss (above), once more arrested in his Chesterfield coat and charged with vagrancy in 1936. Valentine had wished to make an example of the pursed-lipped thug from Brownsville, Brooklyn, but Strauss's brutal exploits over the next five years were of an enormity that the commissioner himself could never have predicted. Valentine certainly approved of the final outcome, however, as both Strauss and Harry "Happy" Maione (below) would burn in the electric chair for their crimes—Maione for the garish cleaver killing of George "Whitey" Rudnick and Strauss for the murder and torching of Irving "Puggy" Feinstein two years later. (Both, author's collection.)

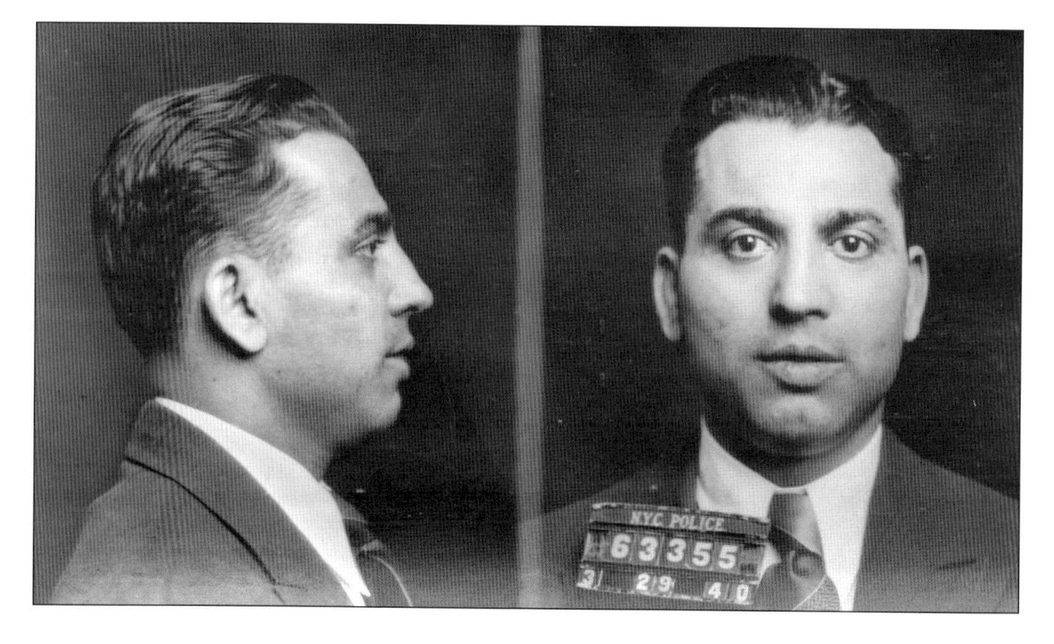

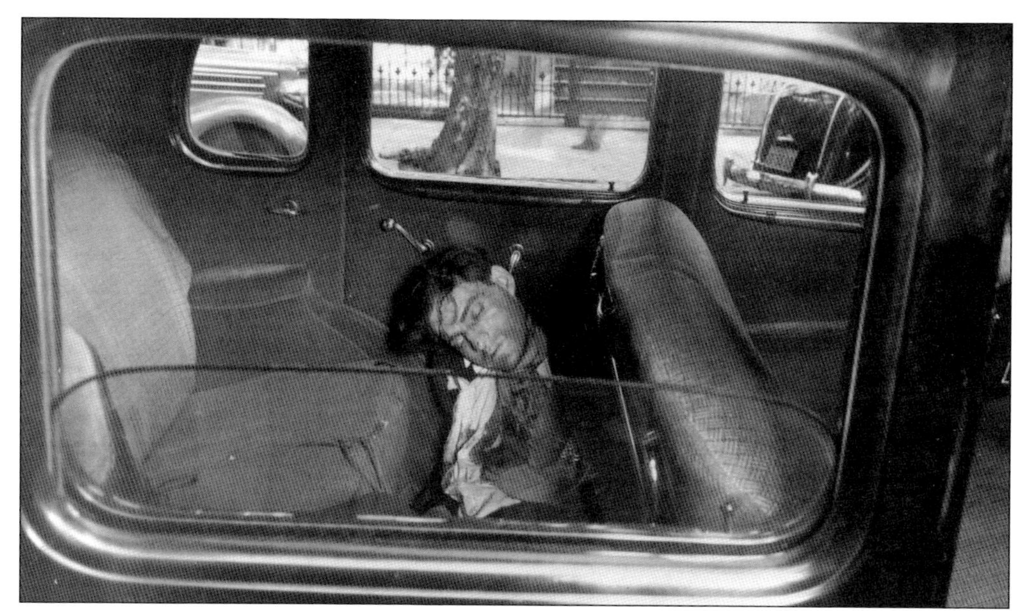

The next and final stop was likely Potter's Field for George "Whitey" Rudnick, a fundamentally insignificant cog in the Brownsville murder machine who died in a fit of violence, the intensity of which was typically reserved for more noteworthy gangland figures than he. Two primary bloodletters for Murder, Inc. would pay a high price in Sing Sing Prison's electric chair for what was described in trial testimony as their giddy demeanor while repeatedly subjecting Rudnick to a meat cleaver and ice pick, then planting a note in his pocket insinuating he had cooperated with the King's County district attorney. If, in fact, Rudnick ever aspired to inform on Louis "Lepke" Buchalter, that ambition ended May 25, 1937, in the back of this stolen automobile, seen discarded along Jefferson Avenue in Brooklyn. (Both, author's collection.)

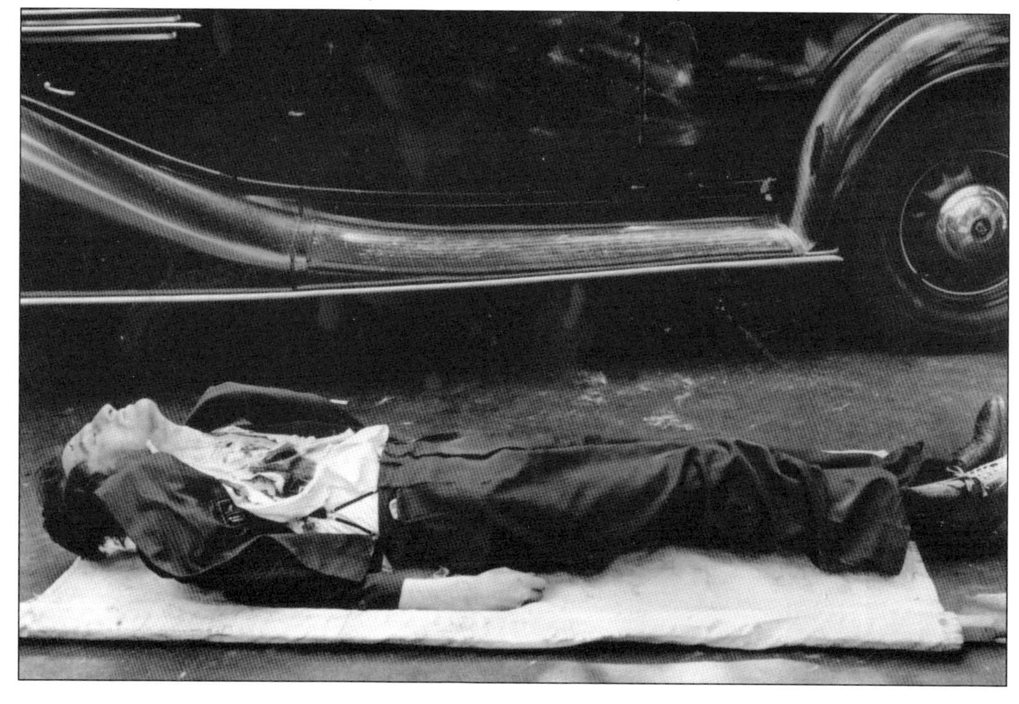

Irving "Puggy" Feinstein was a retired club boxer, a no-account gambler, and an associate of the same Murder, Inc. killers who eventually took his life. On September 5, 1939, Feinstein was tied to a wooden chair, strangled, and ice picked by Abraham "Kid Twist" Reles and Harry "Pep" Strauss. His trussed body was then driven to a vacant lot near the Brooklyn Navy Yards, doused with a can of gasoline, and set alight. In these jarring images preserved within the files of Brooklyn prosecutor Burton B. Turkus, Irving "Puggy" Feinstein's charred remains are spied by rubbernecking neighbors, a pair of wing-tipped shoes his sole recognizable feature. (Both, author's collection.)

Martin "Buggsy" Goldstein (left) modestly referred to himself as "Public Enemy Number Six" but was among a trio of killers who dispatched Irving "Puggy" Feinstein in 1939, supposedly burning off his own eyebrows when he set flame to Feinstein's corpse. And although his bodyguard, Seymour "Blue Jaw" Magoon (right), was not present to witness the pyrotechnics, Goldstein told Magoon enough about it to make him valuable to Brooklyn prosecutors. At Goldstein's trial, Magoon shed tears on the witness stand while the defendant stood in shackles and pleaded, "Seymour, tell the truth!" Then, turning to face the grand jury box where the district attorney William O'Dwyer himself was sitting, Goldstein babbled incoherently, "This guy is burning me . . . the girls in the spaghetti house!" (Author's collection.)

Boxed candy, soda, and cigars were hardly the most unwholesome fare served at Midnight Rose's, located at the corner of Saratoga and Livonia Avenues in Brownsville, Brooklyn, a regular hangout for the hired guns of Murder, Inc. This previously unpublished image was captured during the same period when Kings County district attorney William O'Dwyer was working to dismantle the killing racket, sending most of its central figures to be electrocuted at Sing Sing Prison. Upstairs from Midnight Rose's sat the perhaps too-stylishly named Hollywood-Royal chow mein palace where Jewish and Italian assassins would take in Chinese American dinners for considerably less than the monthly stipend they received from Louis "Lepke" Buchalter. (Author's collection.)

When Louis "Lepke" Buchalter decided to seize a flour truckers' union in 1934, he sent gunman Murray Goldis to do the "big job" on teamster president William Snyder inside Garfein's kosher restaurant. He then installed the killer's brother as the new union delegate. But in July 1938, Buchalter was on the run and sent this hand-scrawled threat to the Goldis family. "If Murray Goldis talks," an NYPD detective recalled a prior warning, "his daughter's throat would be cut from ear to ear." (Both, author's collection.)

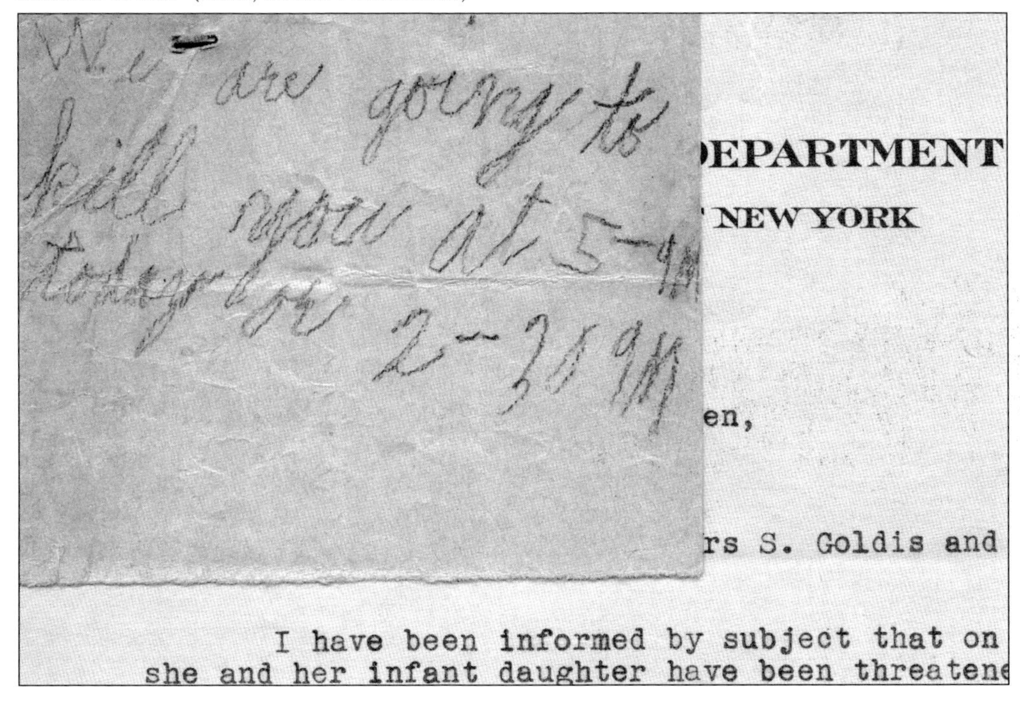

We are going to
kill you at 5 [illegible]
today or 2-3 PM

DEPARTMENT

NEW YORK

en,

rs S. Goldis and

I have been informed by subject that on
she and her infant daughter have been threaten

This would be a typical Brownsville street if not for a view of the candy store once operated by Murder, Inc. victim Joe Rosen. Converted to sell lighting fixtures, Rosen's killers carried an altogether different variety of hardware in September 1936 as they crouched in a hallway across the street to await his arrival. (Author's collection.)

It is unclear if the ice pick at top right in this rare image belonged to the killers of Joe Rosen or to the shop's proprietor himself, seen executed amid copies of the morning's *New York American*. Regardless, 18 bullets proved lethal enough to silence any testimony that Louis "Lepke" Buchalter feared Rosen might deliver to the King's County district attorney. (Author's collection.)

Above, Kings County's star prosecutor, Michael F. Vecchione, holds a hot-wired ignition switch preserved as evidence from the getaway car used in the murder of Joe Rosen. Anthony "Duke" Maffetore admitted stealing the vehicle, which was driven from the crime scene by a fellow witness for the Brooklyn district attorney, Sol "Sholem" Bernstein. Louis "Lepke" Buchalter's paranoia insisted Rosen's testimony would incriminate him, but instead it was Rosen's killing that spelled the end of Lepke's empire. (Photographs by Arthur Nash.)

Purchased by Louis "Lepke" Buchalter in exchange for control of Joe Rosen's labor union, the Sutter Avenue candy store turned very little profit, leaving Rosen unable to support his family and generally dissatisfied with the bargain he had struck. Buchalter allegedly prodded Rosen to leave town, later ordering his death after Rosen stubbornly returned to the Brownsville neighborhood.

Although no evidence exists that Rosen cooperated with the Brooklyn district attorney, it was this murder conspiracy that ultimately condemned Buchalter, called "America's Most Dangerous Criminal," to die in the electric chair at Sing Sing Prison three years after the Murder, Inc. gunmen who carried out his orders. (Author's collection.)

"Are you fellows missing any witnesses?" the live-in manager of the Half Moon Hotel gingerly asked one of several policemen guarding the occupants of a sixth-floor safe house. Moments earlier, he recognized the body of Abe "Kid Twist" Reles laying just feet from a military draft office on the ground level and took it for granted that Reles had gone AWOL from the district attorney's brigade of stool pigeons. Here the man responsible for unraveling Brooklyn's most complex organized crime cases reviews evidence exhibits with Leonora Gidlund of the NYC municipal archives, including the original window latch from the hotel room beneath Reles's own. (Photographs by Arthur Nash.)

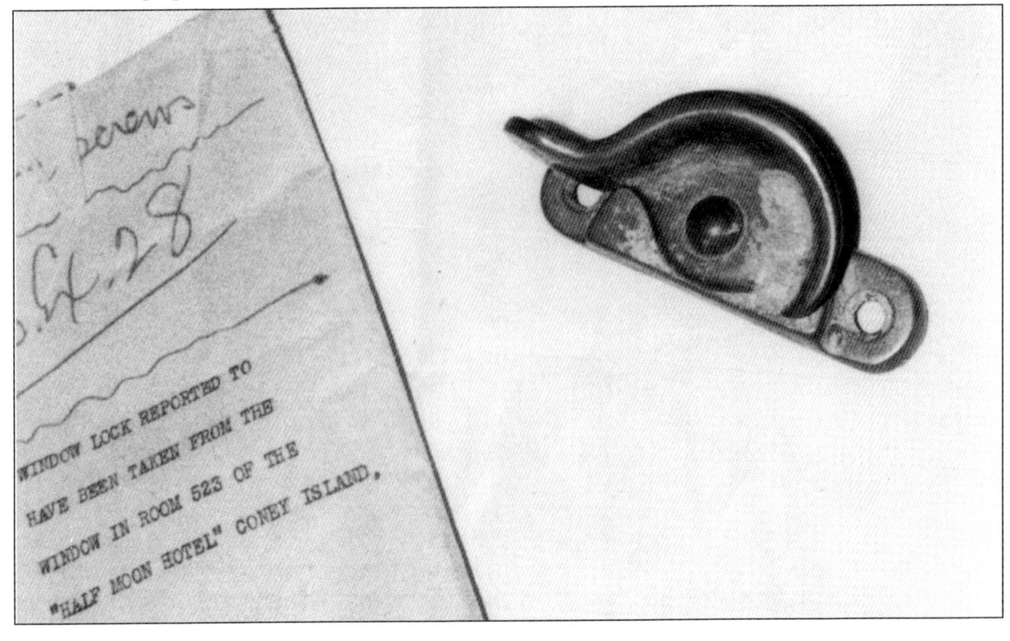

Those skeptical of the Abe Reles escape theory have consistently pointed out that the bed linens Reles allegedly tried to use as a rope ladder—seen in the custody of latex-gloved rackets prosecutor Michael F. Vecchione—were far too short to permit his getaway from the Half Moon Hotel's sixth-floor safe house. When Reles's body was transferred to the morgue and the contents of his hotel bedroom cleared out, the lengths of bedding were placed for safekeeping in the dead man's own valise, where they awaited an official inquest. (Photograph by Arthur Nash.)

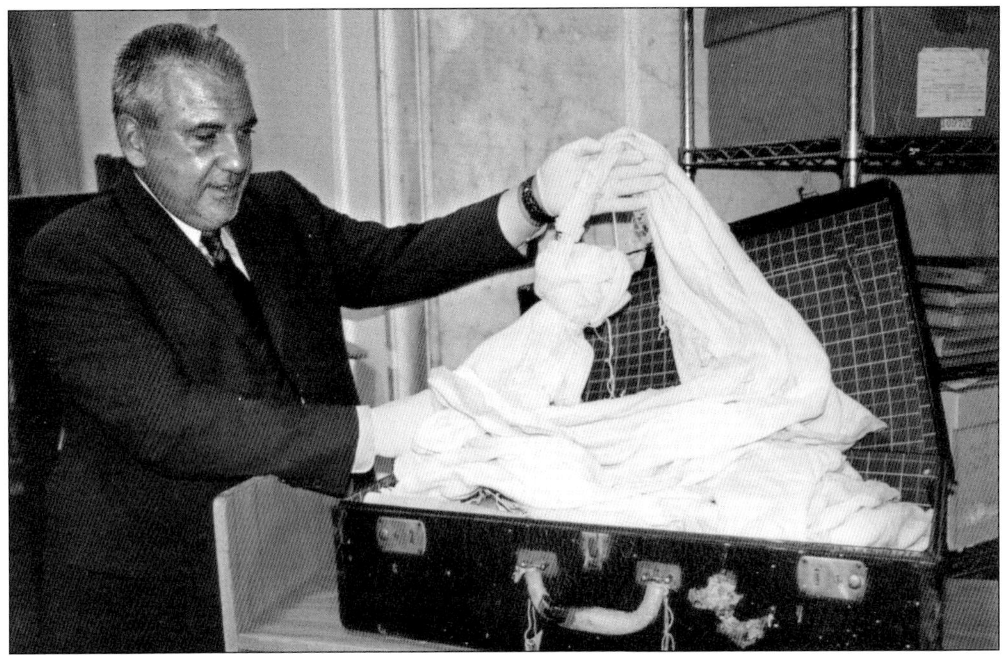

For virtually the first time since the 1940s, snugly knotted bed sheets recovered from the Half Moon Hotel room of Abe "Kid Twist" Reles, razzed posthumously by newspapermen as "The Canary Who Couldn't Fly," are examined. Over nearly seven decades, the circumstances of Reles's demise have been saturated by conjecture; one version maintains that Reles was pitched from his sixth-floor window (below) by members of the police unit assigned to guard him while others insist Reles attempted escape or was playing a practical joke. (Above, photograph by Arthur Nash; below, author's collection.)

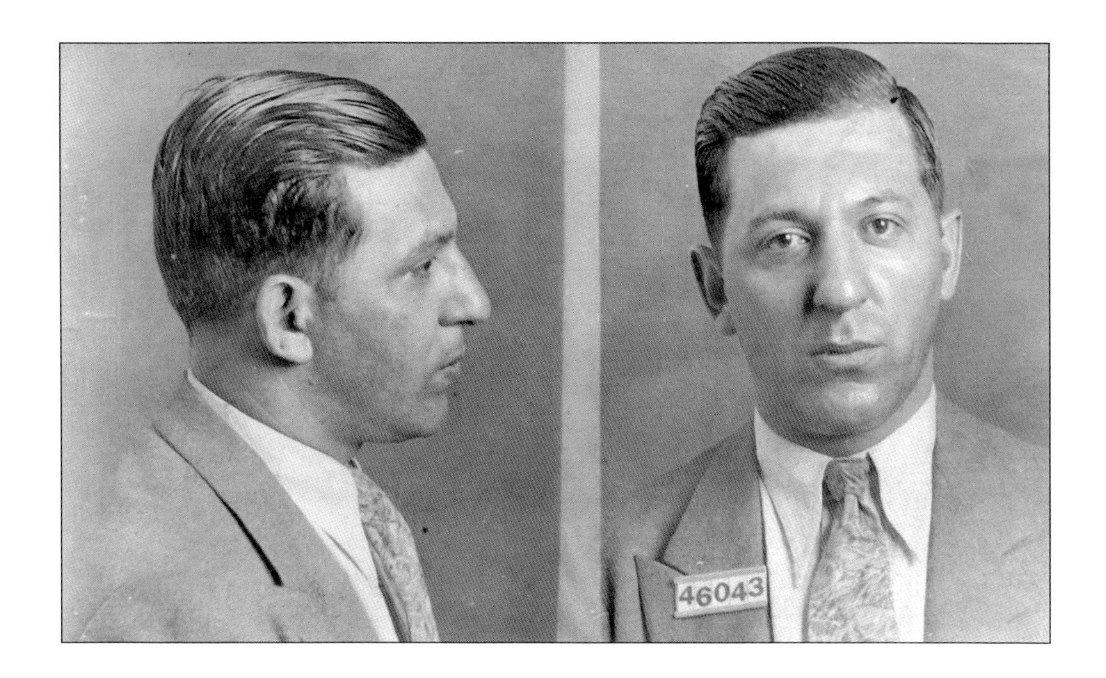

Louis "Lepke" Buchalter (top) and Sol "Sholem" Bernstein (below) occupied radically different ends of the "Kosher Nostra" food chain; one sat on the board of directors of a national crime syndicate and the other was a simple getaway driver, only a step or two above the errand-boy position he had formerly held within the Dutch Schultz gang. But it was Bernstein's testimony during the trial of Joe Rosen's killers that helped seal Buchalter's fate. Bernstein, who drove Rosen's killers to safety but later snubbed a direct order to murder underworld defector Irving "Big Gangi" Cohen, received a suspended sentence. (Both, author's collection.)

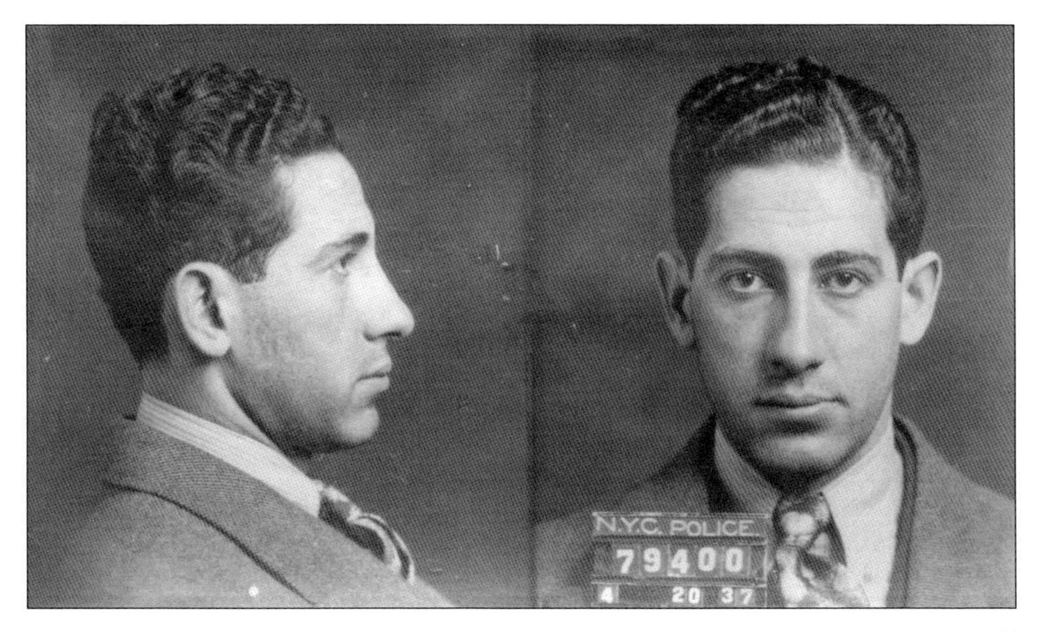

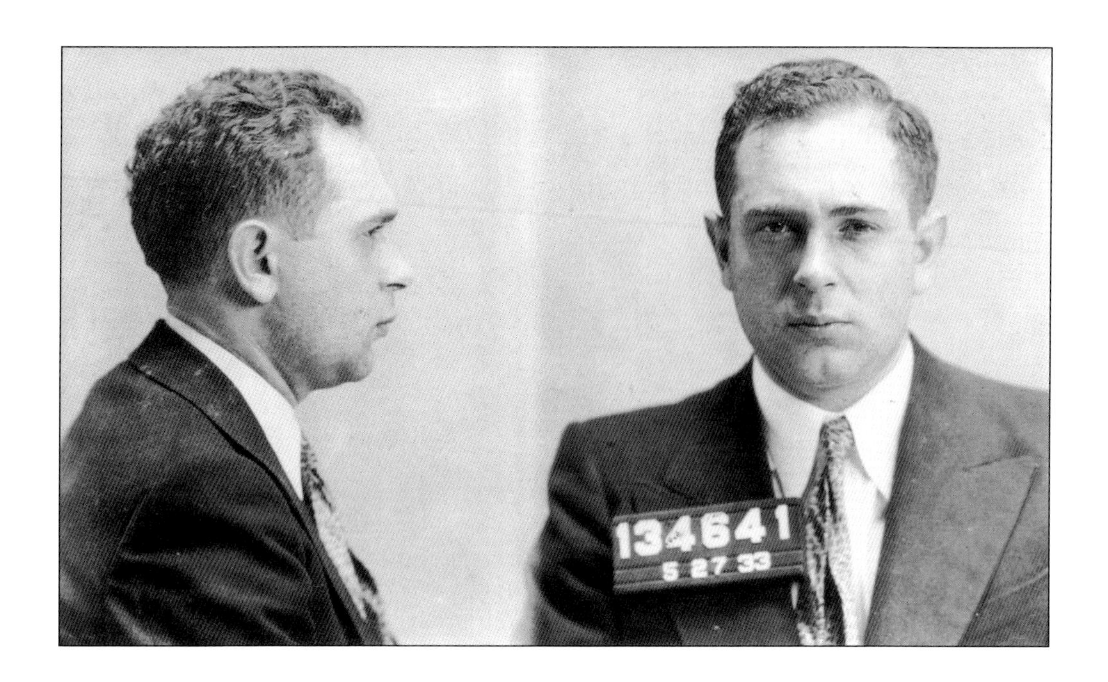

Philip "Little Farvel" Cohen, booked as "Jack Kofsky" in 1933, was among the Murder, Inc. gunmen initially indicted by the Brooklyn district attorney for their roles in Joe Rosen's murder. Unlike the district attorney's immunized witnesses, like getaway driver Sholem Bernstein, Cohen would never actually mount the witness stand against his former bosses; even so, the Rosen murder charges would be dismissed, and instead, Cohen pleaded guilty to a far lesser charge of smuggling heroin from Canada. Meanwhile, fellow informant Abraham "Pretty" Levine (below) would face no punishment at all. (Above, author's collection; below, Avi Bash collection.)

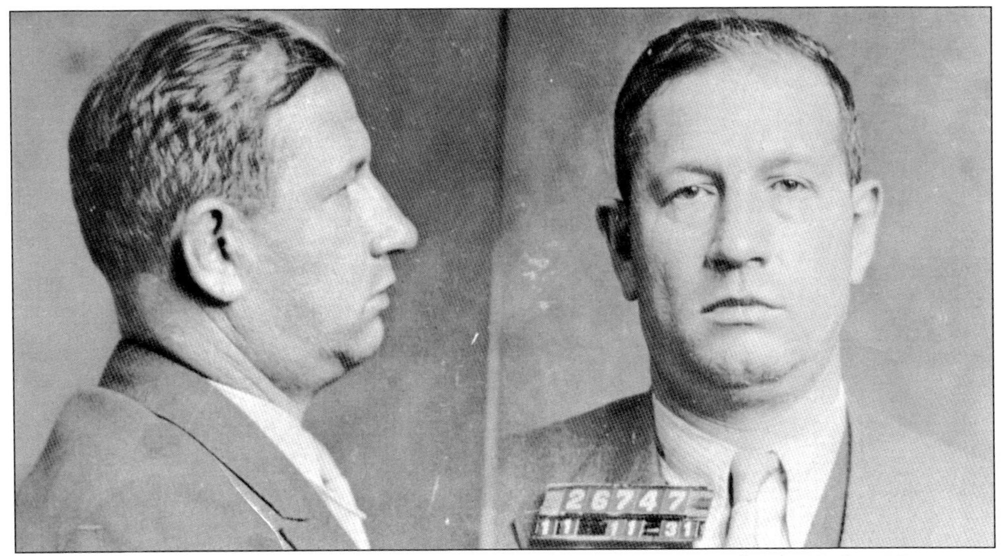

The testimony of cooperating witnesses like Abe "Kid Twist" Reles and Sol "Sholem" Bernstein also shed light on high profile but as yet unsolved gangland slayings such as that of Harry "Big Greenie" Greenberg (above), a lumbering Jewish triggerman who was killed in Los Angeles by Benjamin "Bugsy" Siegel and Frankie "The Wop" Carbo after he made lightly veiled threats to provide evidence against the Brooklyn murder racket. (Author's collection.)

Frankie "The Wop" Carbo, seen in an early arrest photograph, split his time between New York City and Philadelphia as a hired gun for Murder, Inc. To the disappointment of the Kings County district attorney, the Coney Island death plunge of Abe Reles spared Carbo and Benjamin "Bugsy" Siegel from claiming their own seats on death row. (Author's collection.)

Irving "Big Gangi" Cohen (above) was charged with the unenviable task of eliminating his close friend, Walter Sage (below), pictured three years before his ice pick murder for allegedly skimming slot machine revenues. Cohen fled but was extradited from Los Angeles, where he had been working as a bit player in motion pictures—an industry then controlled by Cohen's associates from New York City, including Benjamin "Bugsy" Siegel. Following his acquittal in 1941, Cohen immediately returned to Hollywood, raised a family, and resumed an understated career in acting, portraying cold-blooded killers in a dozen films, including *Crime, Inc.*, whose story line was based upon the crime syndicate Cohen so narrowly escaped. (Author's collection.)

Four

Causing a Racket

The Mob Branches Out

Organizing surprise raids on safecrackers and silk thieves was a healthy diversion for Richard E. Enright, the do-good but beleaguered police commissioner of New York City during the first six years of Prohibition, and among the habitual felons caught up in Enright's recurring nocturnal dragnets was Harry Blake, age 58, also known informally as "Connecticut Blackie," an expert handler of explosives.

"I've been going straight," Blackie insisted during a session of forceful interrogation from Enright at the Chief of Detectives office in lower Manhattan, shortly after his release from an Atlanta prison where he had served time for robbing a U.S. Post Office. "I'm making an honest living bootlegging," the convicted yegg man casually admitted to the dumbstruck commissioner, who no doubt believed he had been given the night off from losing the war on gangland's untaxed liquor. "I sell whiskey and beer now, and I'm getting along just fine," Blackie said, rubbing it in a little before cracking facetiously, "There's nothing like reform, boys!"

When a repeal of the 18th Amendment spelled the end of the Volstead Act's social restrictions and of New York City's countless back-room speakeasies, a veritable army of hoodlums with every bit as much criminal audacity as Harry Blake would hardly pause to mourn the loss of their primary revenue stream. Instead, they placed the underworld's trademark versatility on display by expanding all of their comparatively lesser rackets, and convincingly so, like ravenous tentacles penetrating virtually every aspect of life in the Big Apple—with tens of millions of dollars amassed in bootlegging profits to help to finance their insatiable growth. In retrospect, it would appear that the seemingly irrepressible crime wave that swept across New York City during the 1920s and 1930s may have been less eradicated, per se, than it was merely spread thinner between a broader array of illicit operations both within and well beyond the limits of the five boroughs.

Underworld characters mingle with police, merchants, and the Roman Catholic Church in this mid-1930s portrait of the San Gennaro Feast in Manhattan's Little Italy district. The annual rite has been rumored to be dominated by racketeering interests since its inception more than a

century ago. In the 1990s, when Mayor Rudolph Giuliani challenged the mafia's foothold on the lucrative street fair, the cost to taxpayers was more than $100,000 greater than when mobsters installed the *festa*'s traditional lighting displays. (Acquilino family collection.)

CRIMINAL IDENTIFICATION DIVISION
BUREAU OF POLICE
PHILADELPHIA, PENNSYLVANIA

AGE	26	NAME	Benjamin Sagal NO.
WEIGHT	161 1/2	ALIAS	Bennie Segal Siegal
HEIGHT	5-8 1/4	ADDRESS	57 Cannon St New York
COMP.	M. Dark	OCCUPATION	Auto Livery
HAIR	Dk. Brown	CRIME	Susp. Character
EYES	Org + Blue	OFFICERS	Farles, Bennett, Hackett
BUILD	Med.	F. P. C.	

REMARKS: Associates 80421
Arrested 1-5-26, Brooklyn for Rape

DATE

In 1928, when Benjamin "Bugsy" Siegel was arrested in Philadelphia (above) and charged as a "Suspicious Character," chances are good his stopover in the City of Brotherly Love was to hijack the wares of bootlegging rivals. By 1946, however, with Prohibition a faraway memory, Siegel expanded his professional resume to include the first "Million-dollar Nite Club" in Las Vegas, Nevada, according to the inscription on this autographed memento's verso. (Both, author's collection.)

Joseph "Doc" Stacher was a lifelong confederate of major Jewish racketeers like Benjamin "Bugsy" Siegel and Meyer Lansky, as well as a triggerman for gangland's squelched execution squad, Murder, Inc. He is seen here in flamboyant Western attire doing what he did best—managing gaming casinos for the New York City mob. Behind him sit a pair of Jennings slot machines customized for the Flamingo Hotel in Las Vegas, approximately five years after Siegel's untimely death. (Sugerman family collection.)

Salvatore "Sally Burns" Granello (above and below) was the American mafia's eyes, ears, and enforcement arm amid the glitzy casinos of prerevolutionary Cuba, connected to "the very heart of organized crime" according to the U.S. Attorney's Office. Legend has it that as Fidel Castro's guerrilla force prepared to invade Havana, Granello dug a hole, buried millions in mafia profits, and died still plotting to get it back. In 1970, Granello vanished after vowing to retaliate against the gangland murder of his son, allegedly killed for refusing to compensate Washington, D.C., lobbyist Nathan Voloshen, who arranged special privileges during the elder Granello's imprisonment for tax evasion. (Both, private collection.)

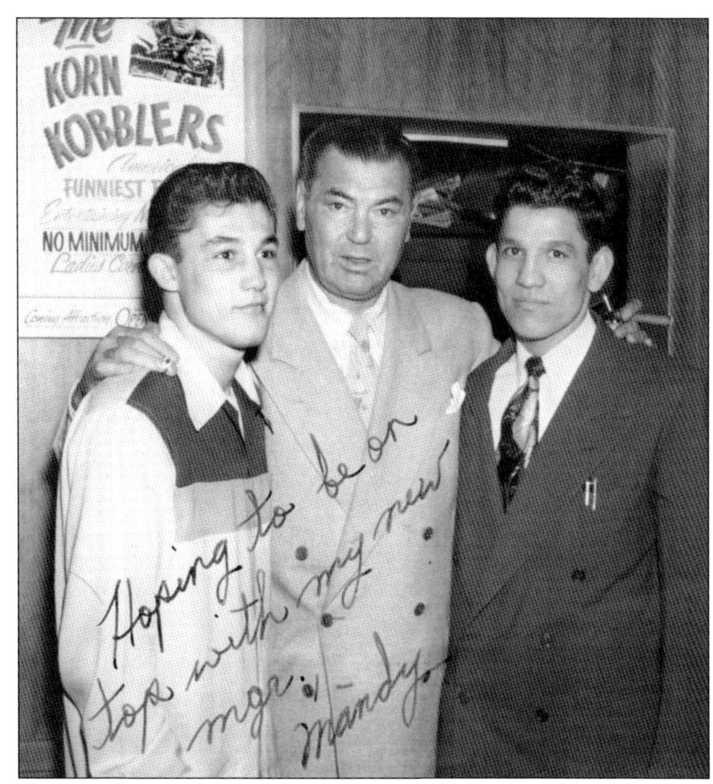

Frankie "The Wop" Carbo's protégé Frank "Blinky" Palermo was adept at fixing prize fights, drugging fighters he managed, and carrying out threats of violence against those who did not "go along." In this image from the estate of Palermo's business partner, Samuel Margolis (below, second row, far left), two of Palermo's freshest ring prospects are seen posing with gangster-friendly former heavyweight boxing champion Jack Dempsey inside his Manhattan saloon. Below, Palermo (first row, second from right) has his picture taken with the champ. (Both, author's collection.)

705?-50M-701125(49) 114 No. 433312

City Magistrates' Court of the City of New York (203746)

D. of J. No. CLASSIFICATION 25 M 7

N. Y. P. D. No. RECORD OF CONVICTIONS 4 M

Name	Date	Offense	Disposition	Magistrate	Court	Officer and Precinct
Albert Lombardozzi	6-25-31	DCAbuse	2Das.	Curtis	1B	Ryan Tr(9 A81537
Albert Lombardozzi	9-10-31	Vag.887	20Das.	Folwell	9B	Kenney 68
Albert Lombardozzi	10-15-52	DC2	10-20 30 Day	Bushel Lorne	N	Molony PCO

Carmine Lombardozzi was called "The Italian Meyer Lansky" as a credit to his talent for managing Gambino crime family assets. His rap sheet (above) began during Prohibition and innumerable arrests would follow, including consorting with criminals, contempt of court for refusing to testify against relatives who beat an FBI agent at his father's funeral, and a more pedestrian charge of failing to pay 102 parking tickets. (Author's collection.)

Joseph "Joe Stutz" Tortorici's feud with the NYPD began in 1927 on charges ranging from bootlegging and labor racketeering to vehicular homicide and strong-arm extortion. But Tortorici made headlines when his brother Frank, a Confectioner's Union delegate, encountered problems with "rebellious candy makers" who resented unauthorized dues being deducted from their already meager paychecks. (Author's collection.)

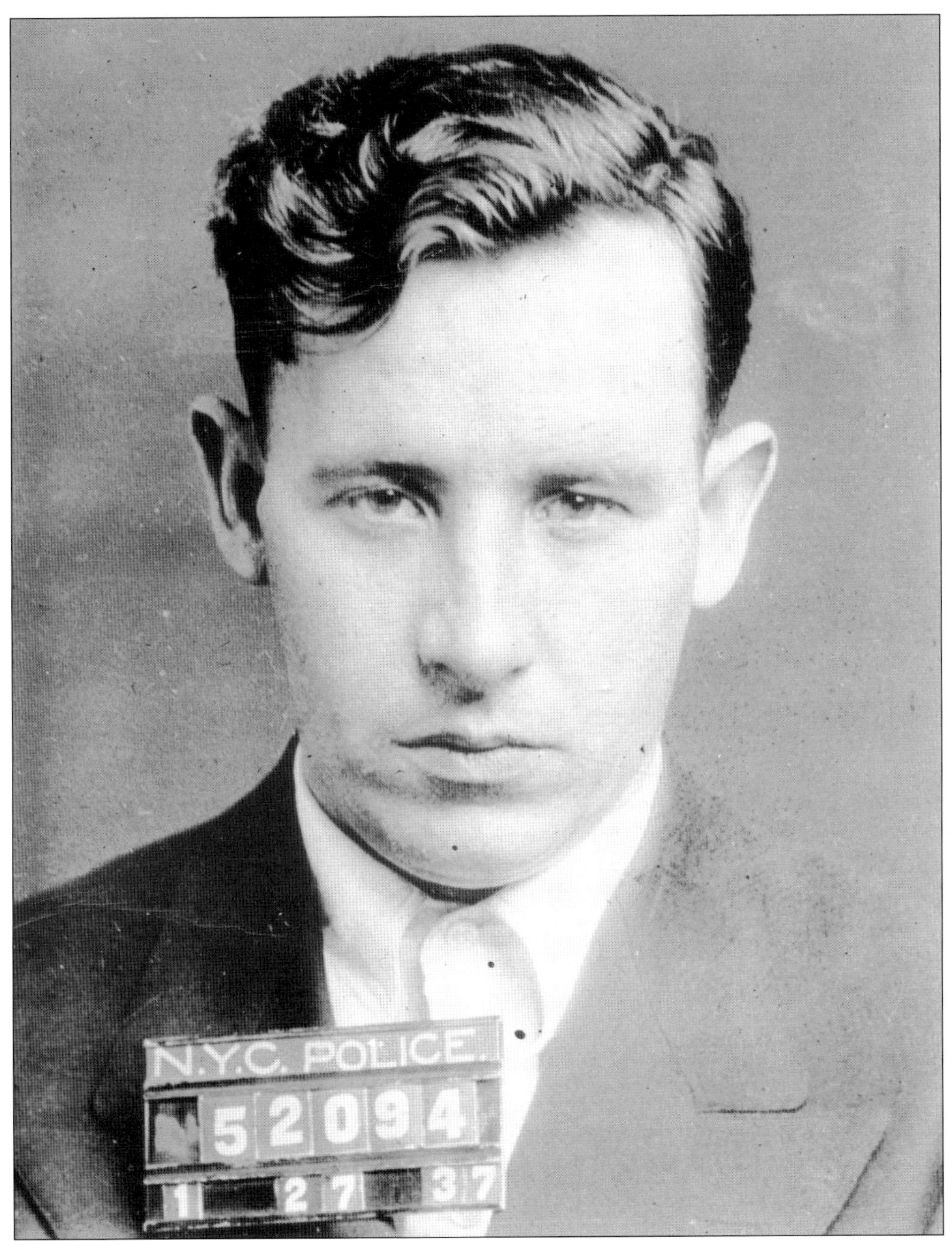

Michael "Mickey" Bowers (above, after violating parole in 1937) was a blue-eyed Irish bank robber who ran an eponymous mob of brass-knuckled hoods until 1940 when the Longshoreman Union's "Pistol Local" delegate, so named because its leaders carried handguns, was killed in Manhattan by an unknown triggerman. Muscling into the vacuum, Bowers surrounded himself with violently deranged men like his cousin "Big Harold" (next page) and shored up control over incoming cargo, as well as the waterfront's lucrative hijacking, smuggling, gambling, and loan-sharking rackets. The Bowers gang commanded an army of stevedores and perfected the threat of work stoppage as a demonstration of power. (Author's collection.)

After years of undisputed domination over the same Hell's Kitchen docks dramatized in Elia Kazan's motion picture *On The Waterfront*, Harold Bowers died of natural causes while still an acting secretary for Union Local 824. The influence of Harold's cousin Michael "Mickey" Bowers was beginning to wear thin by his 1960s automobile collision death, but Mickey's adult son had already been opportunely installed as the new Pistol Local leader and was later elected the union's international president, retiring after five terms and facing allegations he attempted to murder a fellow ILA official. (Author's collection.)

A team of drivers for Ross Trucking Company—the longtime Genovese crime family front—engages in horseplay outside the Jewel Luncheonette on Mulberry Street in Manhattan, later privatized as the Knotty Pine Social Club. In the second row, second from left, is Frank "Soapy Ross" Aquilino, whose family's trucks monopolized the distribution of every banana shipped into New York City. At his left is Mickey Katz, the club's founder. (Author's collection.)

Among the relatively unknown soldiers of New York's underworld was "Soapy Ross" Aquilino (holding infant son), whose day job was driving his father's banana trucks. He maintained anonymity despite his underworld initiation alongside a future boss of the Genovese crime family. Aquilino's activity on the piers was not unnoticed, however, and waterfront investigators concluded, "No one can buy bananas from importers unless they use Ross Trucking." (Aquilino family collection.)

With his back against the wall of Ross Trucking's garage on Mulberry Street in Manhattan, Peter DeFeo (right), also known as the "Mayor of Little Italy," was both the company's "part-time dispatcher"' and its highest paid employee when he was not supplying firearms for gangland shootings. Here the seldom-photographed DeFeo poses with his nephew, future Hollywood actor Frank "Butch" Aquilino, on the day of his First Holy Communion. (Aquilino family collection.)

"Close but no Cigar" may describe this portrait of Frank "Butch" Aquilino (far left), all grown up and laboring at Pier 13, which was controlled by his uncle Peter DeFeo. With him are Jimmy Griffo (center), another uncle, whose brother died in gangland violence, and Carmine Aquilino, who was named by prosecutors during a John Gotti trial. Not a gangster, he was misidentified by detectives observing the Ravenite Social Club. (Aquilino family collection.)

A speakeasy during Prohibition, Club 82 (above) became a popular bacchanal that showcased revues of flamboyantly cross-dressing males mixed with authentic female performers. For 12 years, Vito Genovese's seductive wife, Anna, whom he married just days after her first husband was strangled and stabbed on a Greenwich Village rooftop, supervised 82. Anna's brother Peter Petillo was 82's straw man and even married a showgirl. In 1953, the club's manager, Steven Franse, was himself found strangled, allegedly because Genovese blamed him for Anna's decision to divorce him and, in doing so, expose preciously guarded secrets about his underworld empire. In the souvenir portrait below, two chicly dressed associates of Genovese waterfront soldier Joseph "Jo Jo Crumb" Tedeschi enjoy a night out at Frank Costello's Latin Quarter nightclub. (Both, author's collection.)

Joseph "Jo Jo Crumb" Tedeschi (above, far left) attends the Latin Quarter with friends and associates, including Carlie DiPietro (above, second from right) who was soon after convicted in one of the largest heroin smuggling operations in U.S. history. Tedeschi, whose formerly ruler-straight snout was mashed by an NYPD patrolman, maintained an active presence on Manhattan's waterfront until 1971 when he and seven others, including Columbo organization scion Carmine "Junior" Persico, were charged with intimidating legitimate merchants earning a living on the piers. Afterward, Tedeschi concentrated on collecting from the street vendors of the San Gennaro Feast in Manhattan's Little Italy. Below, Tedeschi and DiPietro (both seated on the left) get connected at a popular gangland watering hole, the Copacabana. (Both, author's collection.)

ILA president Thomas "Teddy" Gleason (in glasses) vowed to rid the waterfront of gangland influence but was roundly criticized for his own ties to organized crime, which preserved its stranglehold on commercial cargo. In this image from Pier 36, Gleason glad-hands with underworld associates, including Harry Lombardi (far left), waterfront muscle Eubie Belice, and Luther Carson (with cigar). (Author's collection.)

Easily discernible from disheveled companions, Carmine Galante had a reputation as a lethal enforcer. His primary racket was narcotics, however, and in 1961, he was imprisoned for smuggling heroin. Four years after his parole, Galante was killed for invading a rival's territory. Police found him with another vice—a trademark cigar—theatrically gripped between his teeth. (Author's collection.)

Salvatore "Lucky" Luciano, buoyant in this private snapshot as an exile in Naples, Italy, relaxes at home with longtime girlfriend Igea Lissoni. Luciano spoons grated parmesan, not heroin or

cocaine; nonetheless, he spearheaded the now-infamous "French Connection" drug pipeline from the comfort of his spectacular Italian villas. (Author's collection.)

Perpetually longing for his life in America, Salvatore "Lucky" Luciano, the man for whom *Time* magazine coined the term "Supergangster," whiled away the 1940s and 1950s marketing hamburgers to U.S. servicemen and expanding his interests in global narcotics traffic. All the while, he was slowly but surely losing his foothold on the crime organization that bore his name. (Both, author's collection.)

This unpretentious brick "castle" was typical of innumerable dwellings that dotted the sidewalks of working-class yet gang-controlled neighborhoods like Brownsville, Ocean Hill, and East New York in the borough of Brooklyn. Today the location of a community playground, this address on Dean Street was the boyhood home of future Gambino crime family leader John Gotti and was located within walking distance of the storefronts that, just over a decade earlier, the contract killers of Murder, Inc. employed as their base of operations. (Author's collection.)

Terrariums, a cockatoo, icons of the Virgin Mary, and a baby carriage all surround the Gotti family dining table, evoking a sense of warmth and security that John Gotti was said to later deny had ever existed under his father's roof. Although not approaching the level of opulence that Gotti would surround himself with as a high-ranking mafioso, a quick visual scan of the Gottis' eat-in kitchen reveals certain comforts like a washing machine, a gas range, and a commercial-grade oven. (Both, author's collection.)

While residing here, John Gotti became affiliated with the teenage gangs of East New York that battled over territory, hijacked automobiles, and performed errands for recruiting members of more advanced organizations. Gotti would face his first criminal arrests while living here at home with his parents. He dropped out of school in 1956 to devote himself to street life and became a prominent member of the thuggish "Fulton-Rockaway Boys." These never-before-published images from John Gotti's private album seem to suggest he was given to exaggeration; he allegedly told an associate of his father: "He never did *nothing*. He never earned *nothing*. So we never had nothing." (Both, author's collection.)

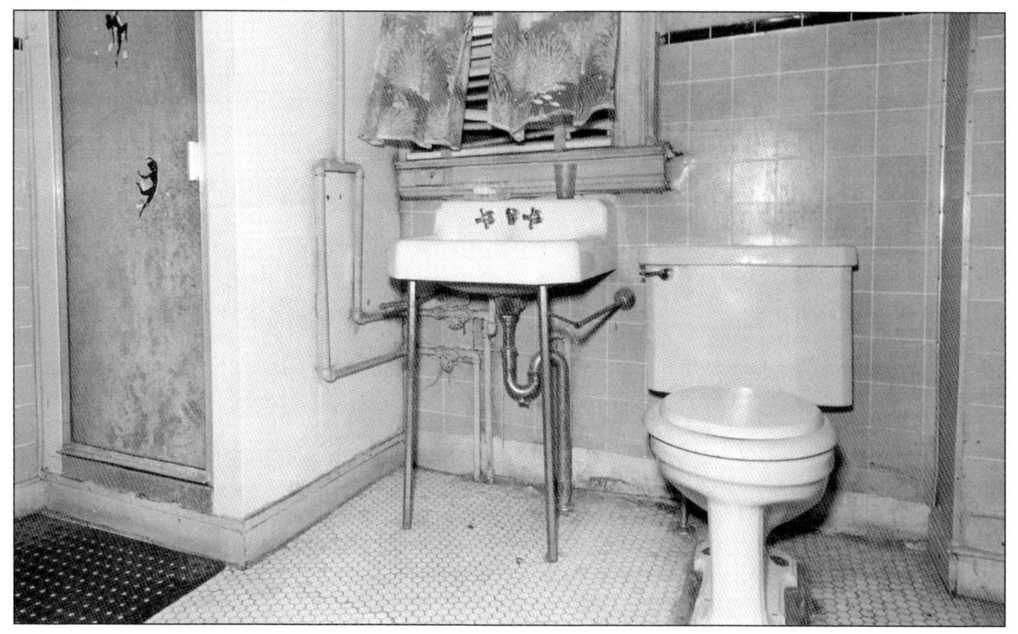

Growing up Gotti was not entirely bad news according to these views of a backyard rose garden and grape vineyard at 2282 Dean Street, which help complete the portrait of John Gotti's upbringing in the tough Brownsville and East New York sections of Brooklyn. Born in the Bronx in 1940, his mother and father's relocation here in 1952 would have a direct and discernable impact upon the Gotti family's respective career paths and enduring public legacy. (Both, author's collection.)

"Economy" was an operative term in the days when young John Gotti and his dozen siblings slept on roll-a-way beds to conserve valuable living space. In the decades that followed, Gotti would abandon all pretense of modesty, taking violent control of the crime organization that in his youth was run by neighborhood gangster Albert Anastasia; moving to an expansive private residence in Howard Beach, Queens; riding in chauffeured limousines; flaunting hand-tailored suits costing thousands of dollars; and generally contributing to his own public ruin. (Author's collection.)

John Gotti and his siblings (including brother Peter, standing in the third row, third from the left) represented a brand new, although not necessarily improved, generation of underworld figures that would usher the Cosa Nostra into the 20th century; they would also set it back exponentially by abandoning many of the traditions set down by racketeers who preceded them. This class photograph was taken in 1953, one year after the Gotti family emigrated from the Bronx to East New York in Brooklyn. (Avi Bash collection.)

Five

Overexposed
Faces of Apalachin

In a midtown Manhattan barbershop on the morning of October 25, 1957, the man most frequently identified by the New York City Police Department as organized crime's anointed "boss" of the Brooklyn waterfront reclined for his customary shave and began making light conversation with second-generation gangland groomer Arthur Grasso when two individuals entered wearing handkerchiefs on their faces and gripping revolvers that, without hesitation, exploded bullishly one after the other into the prone man's massive body. When the gunmen's task was completed, the good fortune of a nationally prominent crime figure was running red beneath tropical pink and blue upholstered chairs, and the future of the underworld empire he helped design was swept into uncertainty.

In the immediate aftermath of Anastasia's murder, key racketeering figures looked to Gotham's prevailing gang leaders for their next move; a gathering would be held on the East Coast, it was decided, to discuss Anastasia's fate as well as how to most equitably divide business interests, including the casino operations reaching from Las Vegas to Havana that the dead man greedily tried to seize a percentage of.

To avoid needless attention from law enforcement, the conference of more than 100 mafiosi would be held northwest of the five boroughs in the tiny community of Apalachin, but an inadvertent brush with local police would prove catastrophic for those in attendance and the spotlight cast on their congregation illuminated a previously unacknowledged fact: that instead of acting as independent agents, gangland factions spanning the nation and globe were actually collaborators working in concert with one another to subvert the law. No longer could federal authorities plausibly deny the existence of crime syndicates.

Thirty-four of the 62 men detained over their involvement with the Apalachin summit originated from the Greater New York City area and an ensuing grand jury investigation revealed their past arrests on charges of gambling, narcotics handling, homicide ("with gun and automobile"), counterfeiting, kidnapping, bombing, obstruction of justice, illegal entry, extortion, bootlegging, felonious assault, burglary, robbery, erasing engine numbers, prostitution, smuggling, and throwing stink bombs.

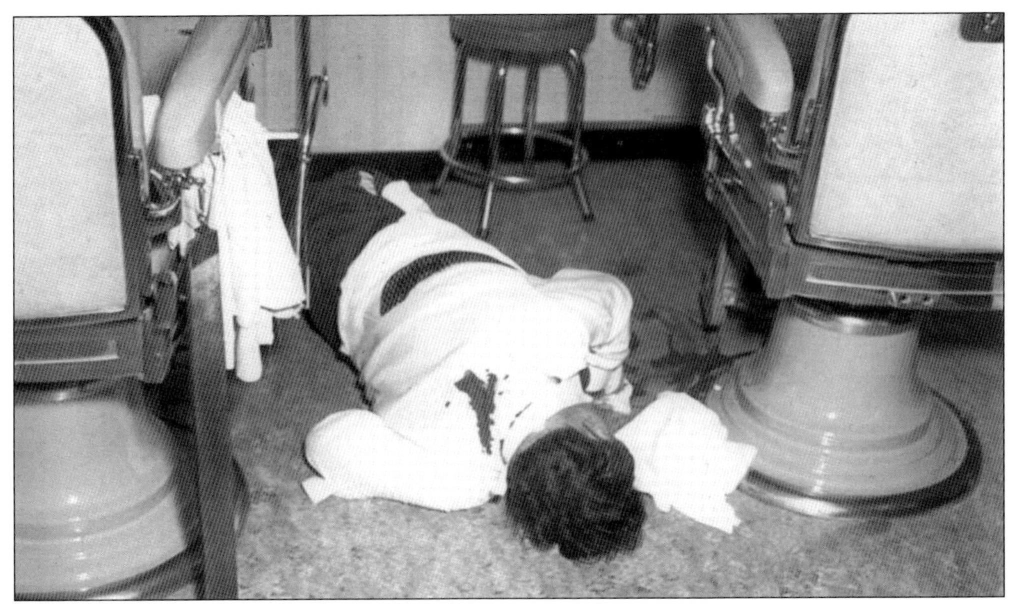

A known hangout for underworld figures, the Grasso family barbershop inside Manhattan's plush Park Central Hotel had already been under police surveillance for more than two decades on the morning that waterfront racketeer Albert Anastasia was finally caught napping by rival gunmen and fell, humbled by their bullets. The fearsome mafia chieftain was no longer the young man whose aptitude for violence helped shape organized crime during the 1920s and 1930s, but he was still powerful enough to shatter an arm of the cast-iron chair from which he made his abbreviated escape. Above, Anastasia is seen exactly as he was found by crime scene photographers from the West Forty-third Street Police Precinct just prior to the arrival of curious newspapermen. (Both, New York City Police.)

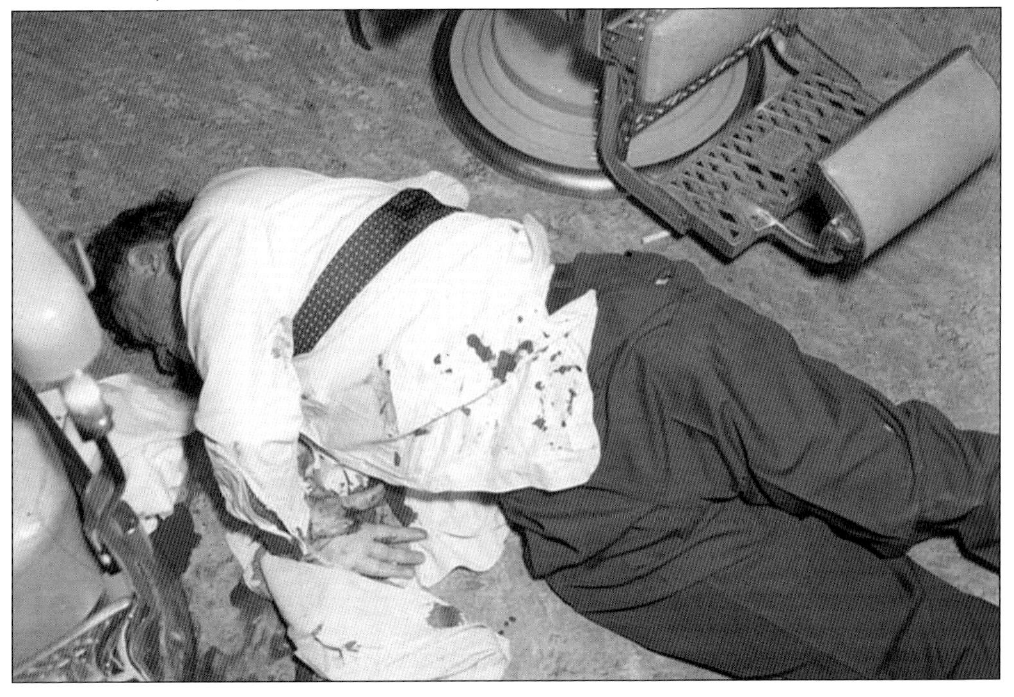

It was perhaps only coincidence that the meeting to discuss Albert Anastasia's brazen murder was hosted by a mafioso nicknamed "The Barber." Yet Joseph Barbara Sr. would sacrifice more than 200 pounds of beefsteak when his houseguests were detained at a state police barracks in November 1957; he would also lose his anonymity once the world was alerted to his reputation as a ranking member of organized crime. Above, the son of "The Barber," Joseph Barbara Jr., sports a finger wave hairstyle as he confers with legal counsel during a post-Apalachin grand jury proceeding. On the right is Barbara family soldier Ignatius Cannone, who arrived late to the party but just in time to spot law enforcement officers staking out the property. (Both, New York State Police.)

During their emigration from Sicily, Russell Bufalino (left) and his family may have chosen the port of entry that sounded most familiar—Buffalo—which is where they put down roots and he launched a career in bootlegging. Bufalino helped make arrangements for the Apalachin meeting and, as luck would have it, the public humiliation caused his boss, Joseph Barbara, to retire, hastening Bufalino's own promotion to the head of his crime family. Longtime Barbara associate Bartolo Guccia (below, during an early-1900s arrest) was sent to investigate the commotion just moments before Bufalino's own car came careening down the driveway. (New York State Police.)

If luxury vehicles fleeing Joseph Barbara's estate were rolling slot machines, the second to reach a state police roadblock held the jackpot—Vito Genovese (above) being spirited away by Russell Bufalino. Although Salvatore "Lucky" Luciano still held sway from exile in Italy, Albert Anastasia's assassination was yet another brazen attempt by Genovese to take over the mafia commission that Luciano founded in 1931. When called to testify before a subcommittee investigating Apalachin in 1958, he stated only that his replies would tend to incriminate him. "By golly they would," responded a committee member, "if you wrote an autobiography." (New Jersey State Police.)

Third in command of the Luciano family was Gerardo "Jerry" Catena, who also tried absconding while crammed in the backseat of Russell Bufalino's Chrysler. Like Vito Genovese, Catena selected to reside in New Jersey and monopolized the vending machine industry with Jewish mob strongman Abner "Longy" Zwillman. Their innumerable enterprises ranged from the Pubic Service Tobacco Corporation to the manufacture of golf shoes. (New Jersey State Police.)

Fourth in command of the Luciano clan, Michele "Big Mike" Miranda was questioned by police about Albert Anastasia's murder and, like several Apalachin participants, he was incarcerated nearly a year for refusing to break his silence regarding the gangland summit. When Genovese was convicted on drug charges and began serving what was ultimately a life sentence, Miranda was promoted within the organization. (New York State Police.)

Joseph Ida led the Bruno crime family of Philadelphia and was actively involved with criminal rackets throughout the tristate area as a close-knit ally of Vito Genovese. Two years after the Apalachin conference, Ida fled the country to avoid a conviction for distributing heroin, while Genovese did not and died in prison. (New Jersey State Police.)

Ida's associate, Dominic Oliveto, was the final passenger sharing Russell Bufalino's getaway car. The company he kept both during and after the Apalachin incident underscored Oliveto's prominence within the Cosa Nostra community for investigators. He would also opt to step aside rather than face ramped-up scrutiny from law enforcement, which inevitably followed the raid. (New Jersey State Police.)

Voted in as Buffalo's "Man of the Year" for 1956, John C. Montana's purported brake failure in a rainstorm landed him on law enforcement's map as the longtime second in command of the Maggadino clan. Montana said he'd "as soon die than plead the Fifth," and lost favor with peers by giving testimony that invoked the names of fellow mobsters, including his partners in a Budweiser distributorship. (New York State Police.)

Hitching a ride with John C. Montana was his uncle by marriage, Anthony "Nino" Maggadino of Niagara Falls, the younger brother of national mafia commission member Stefano "The Undertaker" Maggadino, who, in lockstep with Luciano family underboss Vito Genovese, adamantly ignored Joseph Barbara Sr.'s caveat that his 130-acre ranch was no longer secure enough to host a conference of such magnitude. (New York State Police.)

HOW LONG A RESIDENT OF PRESENT CITY AND S

DATED

FINGERPRINT IMPRESSIONS ON REVERSE SIDE M
ONLY NEED BE SUBMITTED WITHOUT FINGER

On paper at least, James LaDuca was employed as a humble dispatcher for the Van Dyke Cab Company, a multitude of hacks owned by John C. Montana, yet he drove to Apalachin from his stately home on suburban Buffalo's "Mafia Row" wrapped in a coral-and-pink-colored Lincoln coupe. He left the affair on his own two feet, nonetheless, trudging through the sodden forest behind Joseph Barbara Sr.'s estate, much unlike his father-in-law Stefano "The Undertaker" Maggadino, who shrewdly stayed indoors and went undetected because the police officers detaining panicked guests did not have a warrant to search the residence. (New York State Police.)

Of those apprehended fleeing the Barbara estate, 53 percent had prior arrest records involving commerce in illegal alcohol, including glowering Buffalo crime family capo Rosario "Roy" Carlisi (left), while 42 percent had been prosecuted for gambling and 38 percent for murder. To the other extreme, however, 72 percent had been taken in on suspicion of narcotics trafficking. (New York State Police.)

Among the latter group was another Maggadino crime family associate, Dominick D'Agostino of Niagara Falls, seen here in an early U.S. passport portrait. D'Agostino's proximity to the wide-open Canadian border was no mere coincidence; it made shopping for internationally produced heroin, cocaine, and opium as convenient as a trip to the corner market. (Author's Collection.)

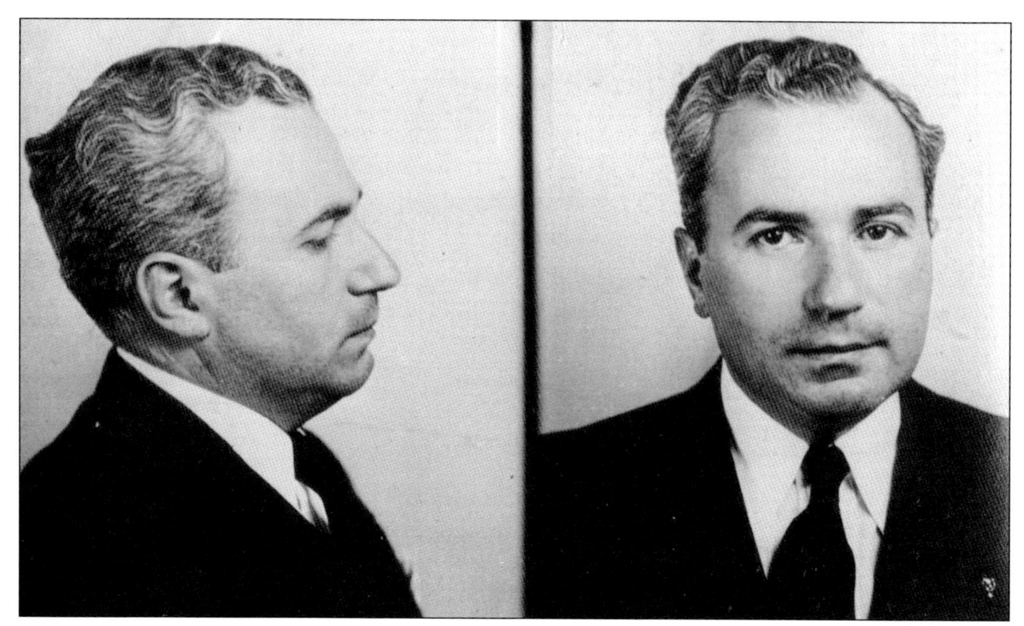

Joseph Falcone (above and below seated far left) was both feared and fabled in the city of Utica, once called the "Sin City of the East." He had once been charged with supplying immense quantities of sugar to untaxed liquor stills after Prohibition and though publicly exposed at Apalachin, the politically connected Falcone remained a powerful force as a senior emissary of the Maggadino clan. Falcone attended the summit with his brother Salvatore, who afterward retired to a produce stand in Miami. By the 1970s, Falcone had become obsolete and reduced to weakly demanding "tribute" tax from bemused local businessmen. Another Apalachin guest sits to Falcone's left in the person of Profaci organization aide Salvatore Tornabe, who avoided a conspiracy conviction by dying of natural causes just weeks after the raid. (Above, author's collection; below, New York State Police.)

Joseph Riccabono (left) and designated driver Paul Castellano were among the entourage accompanying mafia commission member Carlo Gambino to the village of Apalachin. Gambino, who allegedly conspired with Vito Genovese to eliminate Albert Anastasia, insisted, as did most attendees, that he was in town to visit an old friend, Joseph Barbara Sr., who had fallen ill. (New York State Police.)

Paul Castellano (right) and Joseph Riccabono would each spend seven months in jail for refusing to answer more detailed questions about their presence on the Barbara estate. Another of the Gambino clan, Carmine "The Doctor" Lombardozzi told the state police that he was there on a wild game safari in spite of his wide brimmed hat, "pointed shoes," and lack of a hunting rifle. (New York State Police.)

Vincent "Nunzio" Rao (right) and Giovanni "Big John" Ormento were senior representatives of the Lucchese organization at Apalachin. Veteran East Harlem gangsters presiding over the violent "107th Street Mob" of narcotics peddlers, they openly plied their trade while generating hundreds of millions in profit. The distribution ring was done in following Apalachin by the indictment of Ormento and 18 other associates, including future Bonanno clan leader Carmine Galante. (New York State Police.)

Giovanni "Big John" Ormento (left) was an ally of Apalachin's primary talking point, Albert Anastasia, but the Cosa Nostra's most prominent "babbania" smuggler also had business to discuss with Anastasia's executioners. This included the new Federal Narcotics Act, which stiffened penalties even for first-time drug offenses. Ormento would never have that conversation and, like Vito Genovese, spent the rest of his life imprisoned for conspiring to distribute heroin. (New York State Police.)

When the raid began in earnest, DeCavalcante crime family representatives Francesco "Big Frank" Majuri (left) and Louis Anthony LaRasso abandoned their 1956 Chrysler where it sat and made a beeline away from the Barbara estate. Three-quarters of a mile down the road, the two were spotted by an unsuspecting motorist while in the act of hitching a ride back home to New Jersey. (New Jersey State Police.)

Louis Anthony LaRasso was a union organizer who sought to mingle with national organized crime figures on behalf of the DeCavalcante organization. LaRasso was one of the very few attendees who, when investigated by the New York State Police, was found to have no prior criminal record. He would, nevertheless, succeed his hitchhiking companion Francesco "Big Frank" Majuri as the DeCavalcante underboss in the wake of Apalachin. (New Jersey State Police.)

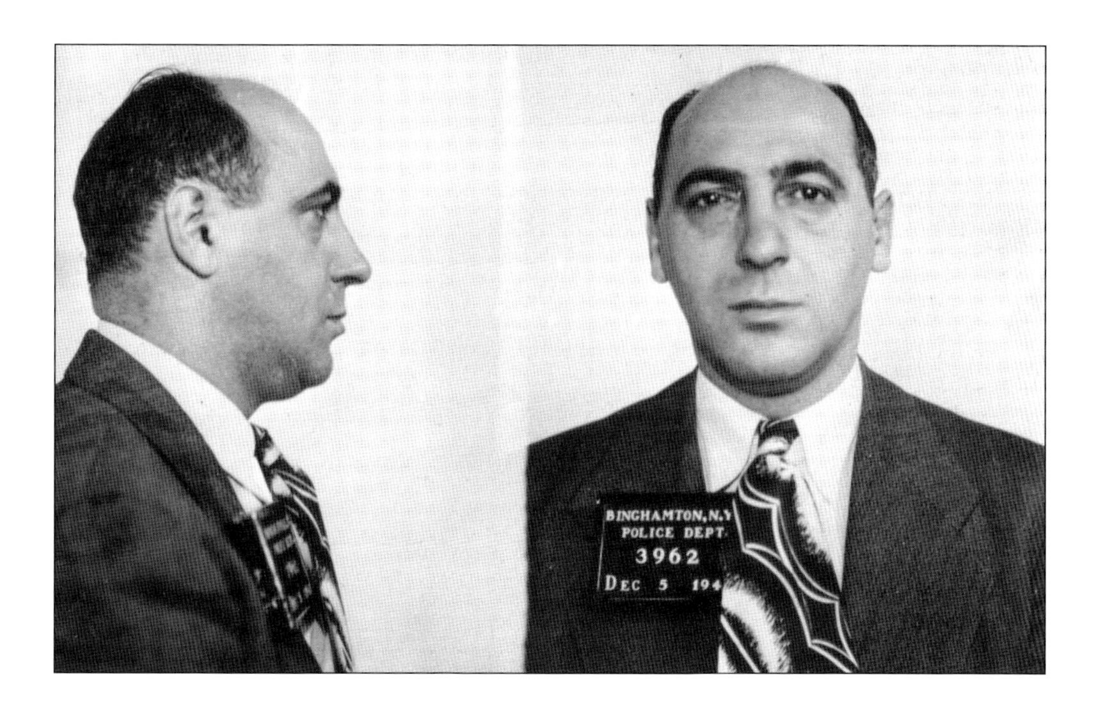

Anthony "The Gov" Guarnieri (above) was said to have been party host Joseph Barbara Sr.'s closest aide and an active garments industry racketeer along the northern tier of New York State; in fact, notice how Guarnieri takes the clothing racket a step further in this 1940s mug shot by draping his extravagantly wide necktie so that it obscures the date of arrest. And Emanuel "Manny" Zicari (below, in a much earlier image) was a Barbara family capo as well, although his legitimate occupation was as manager of Barbara's Canada Dry bottling plant in the village of Endicott, otherwise known as Apalachin. (Both, author's collection.)

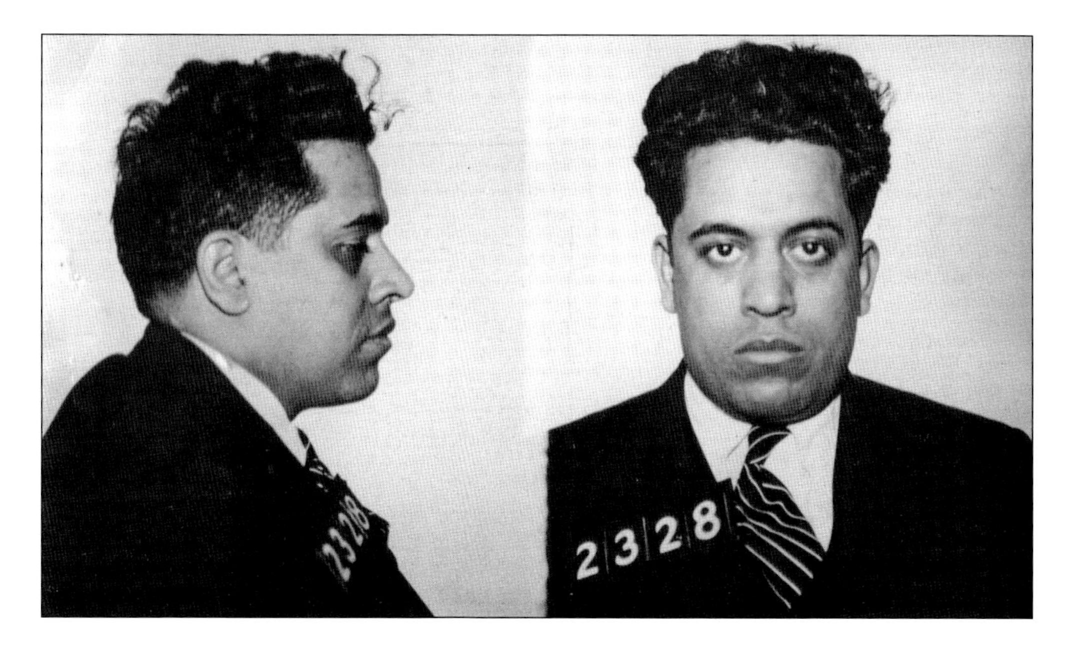

Pasquale "Patsy" Turrigiano was born in the picturesque mafia hotbed of Castellammare, Sicily, but he made his home in remote Endicott, New York, where, he explained under questioning, he worked in the soft drink business. Turrigiano was one of five who admitted to sharing the same profession, a group outnumbered only by dress manufacturers and vending machine operators. There were also five union organizers, four beer distributors, and three cheese importers while two men admitted to gambling for a living. Perhaps having a laugh at law enforcement's expense, a bubbly Turrigiano answered the grand jury's summons with dried mud caked on his wing-tips. (New York State Police.)

RESTRICTIONS

VALID FOR ☒ ONE ENTRY ONLY ☐ MULTIPLE ENTRIES

1. This document is not valid for return to the United States after a temporary absence in: any country except France, Italy, Israel, Austria, Germany or Switzerland.

2. In addition this document is not valid for return to the United States after a temporary absence in any of the following countries unless this restriction is specifically waived with regard to any such country or countries by indorsement hereon:

Bulgaria
Czechoslovakia
Estonia
Hungary
Latvia
Lithuania
Outer Mongolia
Poland
Rumania
Soviet Zone of Germany ("German Democratic Republic")
Union of Soviet Socialist Republics
Yugoslavia

The above restriction is waived as to the following: ______

Joseph Stacher

"All members of this so-called Syndicate are Italian and the overwhelming majority has roots in Sicily," wrote James J. Doyle of the state police in his statistical report on Apalachin, which did not account for Jewish gaming czar Joseph "Doc" Stacher (above), who was invited but did not attend. All but nine that did had criminal records, and out of 275 aggregate arrests, they faced conviction just 100 times. Doyle also calculated that only two of the lavish automobiles stopped by roadblocks were more than three years old; the pristine black Cadillac carrying future Bonanno crime family boss Natale "Joe Diamond" Evola (right) was not among them, however. (Above, Sugerman family collection; right, New York State Police.)

National commission member Joseph Bonanno was quick to join the choir of mobsters warning his cousin Stefano "The Undertaker" Maggadino that the estate of Joseph Barbara was no longer a suitable meeting place. When the raid began, a panicked Bonanno tried escaping on foot through a cow pasture but was intercepted by the state police a short distance away, where he denied having been present on the property. (Marnix Brendel Collection.)

"Joseph Profaci is among the most powerful underworld figures and we expect to develop that information," commented Robert F. Kennedy during Senate hearings on Apalachin in 1958, frustrated by the olive oil importer's suddenly molasses-thick accent and deliberate erection of a language barrier. "We would do this more successfully," Kennedy continued mockingly, "if Mr. Profaci would answer the questions." (New York State Police.)

Six

The Godfather Game

Gangland Jumps the Shark

On a crisp spring morning in 1972, the man nominated by newspapermen as most likely to have shot Albert Anastasia and who Robert Kennedy haltingly praised as "the toughest hood I ever met" strode into the office of a prominent physician in Manhattan and, breezing past the receptionist, brandished a black violin case that he had been clutching beneath one arm. Within it lay a Thompson automatic rifle—the dreaded Tommy Gun—or, at minimum, a popular new board game designed to resemble one.

At FAO Schwartz in midtown, The Godfather Game was among the newest releases—not unlike its purchaser, freshly paroled from Auburn State Prison. In motion picture houses throughout the five boroughs, meanwhile, cinephiles immersed themselves in Marlon Brando's mumbling, often incoherent, portrayal of fictitious gangster Don Vito Corleone. This man had gone to see it, too—he couldn't refuse—and had seen a lot worse.

But now, from a coat pocket that in the not-so-distant past might have held a loaded handgun, he instead yanked a ballpoint pen, and across the game board's face he scrawled: "To My Mouthpiece" then beneath it, "Joey Gallo," before handing it lock, stock, and barrel to the dental surgeon who had sculpted his impossibly large veneers and introduced the notorious Brooklynite to his new bride—a chaperone through his post-penitentiary world of celebrities, social scenes, and limelight under which most men of his chosen profession had a propensity to wilt.

"Crazy" Joe Gallo left 10 years of confinement just in time to watch gangland "jump the shark," in television-land jargon, then usher in a generation of willful, would-be wiseguys and their inescapable mantra, "Fuggeddaboudit," that satirized the underworld's long-tempered customs, steadily diluting traditions that separated their secret subculture from the realm of ordinary criminals, shielding it from exposure. What the police and their evolving technology could never fully achieve was in some respects accomplished by the flamboyant self-parody of the hoods who outlived Gallo, like the so-called "Teflon Don," and by the law of diminishing returns.

Gunslingers from Red Hook, Brooklyn's waterfront, the Gallo clan still bore allegiance to Joseph Profaci when these portraits were taken inside the Copacabana nightclub where, two decades later, their charismatic leader "Crazy" Joe Gallo would celebrate the final few hours of his violent but eventful life. Seated at far left is the youngest Gallo brother, Albert Jr., and at the far end of the same table, seated fourth on the left, is the eldest brother, Larry "Big Boy" Gallo. (Author's collection.)

Seated in the other half of this gangland panorama is the Gallo family patriarch, Albert Sr. (foreground, left), and his wife, Mary Gallo (on his left), while their jovial son Larry can be spotted peeking between them (back row, to the left of the mirror). Across the table, second and third from right, are seated Santo "Uncle Sam" and Gloria Patane, who along with 16 others were indicted on suspicions that they plotted to eliminate 22 members of Joseph Profaci's organization in 1962. (Author's collection.)

"Under New Management" was a slogan that applied itself not only to this Brooklyn eatery, but also to the internal structure of the New York City underworld after the Gallo clan declared war on gang lord Joseph Profaci. At left, Albert Gallo Sr. stands proudly with his youngest son and namesake, Albert Gallo Jr., immortalized as "Kid Blast" in a 12-minute ballad by folk singer Bob Dylan. And below, a swaggering Al Gallo Jr. seems to imitate the swan on the hood of this 1940s Packard, while an unidentified associate eyeballs photographer Jerry Schindlinger. (Both, author's collection.)

Anthony "Tony Bender" Strollo ran Greenwich Village nightclubs for Vito Genovese and was the Gallo brothers' most powerful supporter during their rebellion against Joseph Profaci, but that relationship abruptly ended upon Strollo's kidnapping and murder in April 1962. Born in lower Manhattan, Strollo likely died at this mafia graveyard in Jackson Township, New Jersey, where underworld enforcer Harold "Kayo" Konisberg confessed he sunk Strollo's body in a Prohibition-era whiskey mash pit once owned by Jersey crime figure Joseph "Bayonne Joe" Zicarelli. The FBI unearthed portions of the remote 12-acre chicken farm, seen above and below, in 1967. (Both, author's collection.)

Joseph Celso (left) was convicted in 1964 alongside Harold "Kayo" Konisberg for possessing stolen property, but Konisberg was soon indicted on serious felonies and began cooperating with federal authorities. Fearing the killer known as "King of the Loansharks" might reveal the existence of their burial ground, Celso's superiors ordered him to exhume the bodies of Anthony Strollo and others he helped plant in and around his chicken farm. (Author's collection.)

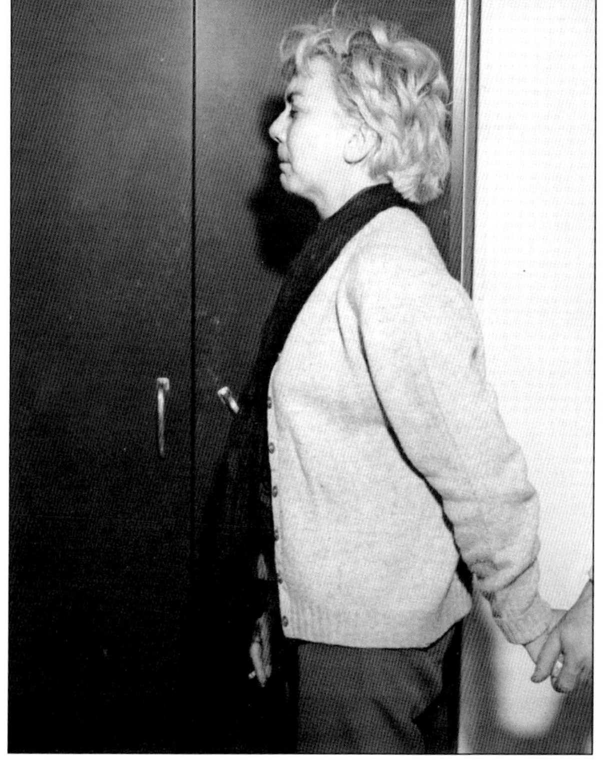

Among the various gangland figures whose bodies the FBI hoped to locate—in addition to Anthony Strollo—were Gallo gang enforcer Joseph "Joe Jelly" Gioelli and two long presumed dead triggermen for the late Albert Anastasia. Seen here is Joseph's wife, Rose, who can hardly enjoy a cigarette while her wrist is persuasively tweaked by a federal agent. (Author's collection.)

In this metal drum beneath a concrete slab in a disused chicken coop, FBI agents discovered one of three sets of skeletal remains that Joseph Celso failed to disinter; none of them belonged to Gallo gang mentor Anthony Strollo. "The code of the Cosa Nostra calls for absolute loyalty", commented FBI director J. Edgar Hoover upon announcing his agents' grisly finds. "And the penalty for betrayal is death." (Author's collection.)

According to the longest prevailing theory, Joseph Profaci (above) was granted authority to kill Albert Anastasia at Manhattan's Park Central Hotel in 1957 with the consent of Vito Genovese and Carlo Gambino; and it was Profaci, seen as he appeared on his 1930s New York City concealed weapons permit, who then awarded the murder contract to "Crazy" Joe Gallo and his team of shooters, whose aspirations were consistently at odds with Profaci's tightfistedness. (Author's collection.)

"These boys are good boys," Sista Biaz told newsmen after the Gallo gang stormed her Brooklyn apartment to rescue six young children from a mattress fire. "Crazy" Joe Gallo's brother Albert Jr. (center) was among the daring participants as well as Frank Illiano (far right) and Anthony Abbatamarco (far left). It was Joseph Profaci's refusal to carve up rackets belonging to Abbatamarco's dead father that instigated warring between the two factions. (Author's collection.)

"When they tried to strangle Larry," Bob Dylan sang, "Joey nearly hit the roof / He went out that night to seek revenge / thinking he was bulletproof." Leaving the site of an iconic double-cross, Larry "Big Boy" Gallo (wearing fedora) walked into a trap but lived to fight another day when the NYPD stumbled upon the ambush; the rope that choked Gallo is held by a detective no doubt frustrated by the underworld's code of silence. (Author's collection.)

Cherub-faced Carmine "Junior" Persico wears a "What, Me Worry?" expression, at least outwardly unconcerned as he is booked inside the Bergin Street Brooklyn Police Precinct on suspicion of killing a longshoreman whose body was found in a South Brooklyn gutter. The slithery 17-year-old Persico was a close confederate of the Gallo brothers but quietly shifted his allegiance to Joseph Profaci's faction shortly before the attempted strangulation of Larry Gallo. (Author's collection.)

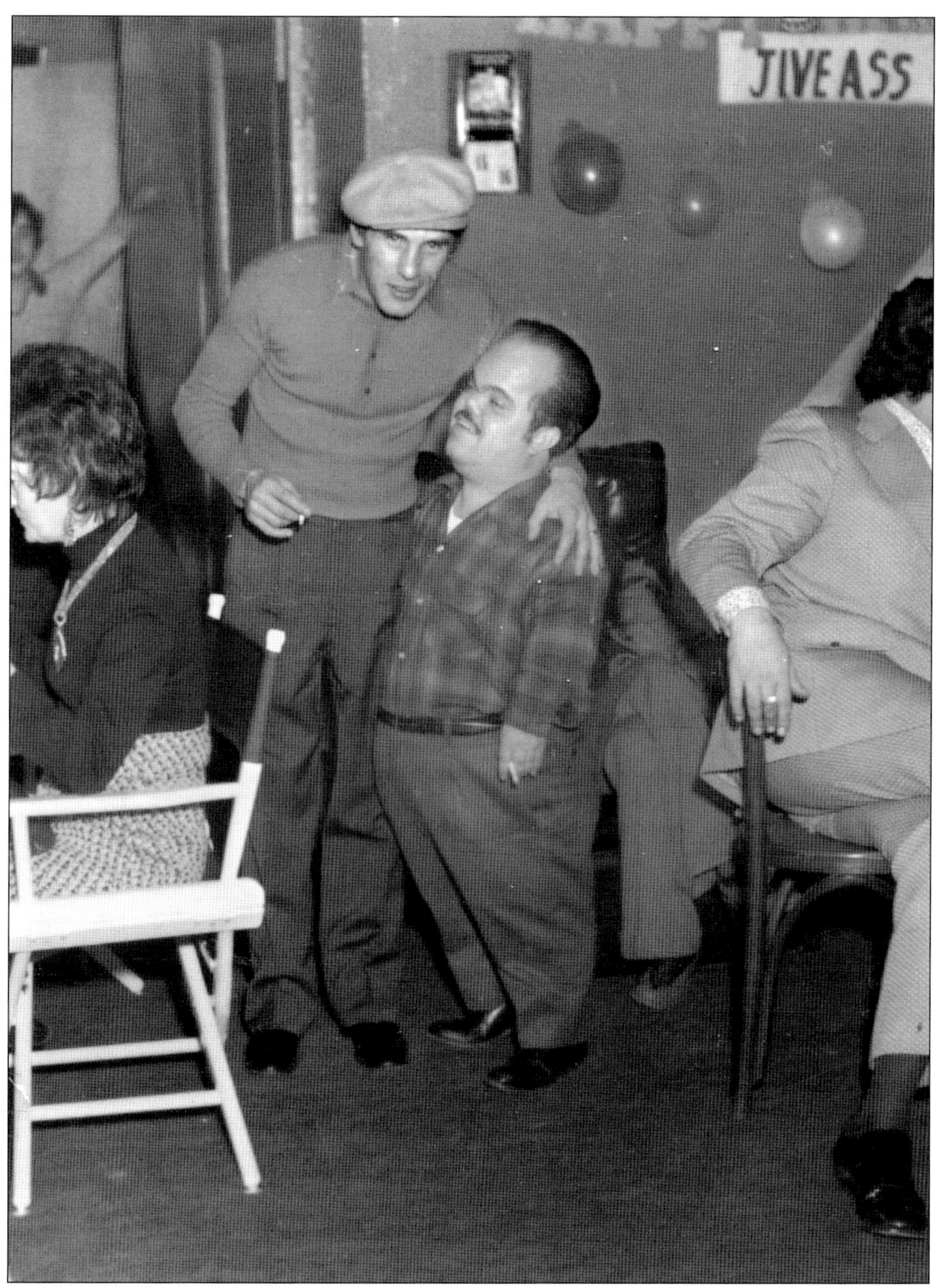

In spite of "Crazy" Joe Gallo's nearly 10-year absence from the streets of Red Hook, he and Armando "Mando" Illiano (right) make a show of camaraderie at a gang-sponsored birthday celebration for Lisa Essary, Gallo's new daughter by marriage. The Gallo clan, most of whom attended the party, welcomed the 10 year old by coating the walls of their headquarters in brilliant yellow, red, and orange. The slogan "Jive Ass," incidentally, was Gallo's playful nickname for the birthday girl. (Author's collection.)

"Crazy" Joe Gallo expresses equally fervent devotion toward his new bride, Sina Essary. The improbable newlyweds met when Gallo noticed Essary working as a dental assistant in the apartment building where they each lived and refused to take "no" for an answer. Before marrying into the mafia, Essary was a single mother from the Midwest who had no familiarity with organized crime or the legion of colorful characters devoted to her enigmatic new husband, like Angelo Parfumi (below). And although he had just recently been paroled from prison, remarried, and then divorced once again, Gallo's longterm plans at the time of his death appeared to revolve around Essary and her thespian daughter, Lisa. Gallo's own mother, Mary, can be seen speaking with her hands as she awaits the cutting of the birthday cake. (Both, author's collection.)

The menagerie assembled in "Crazy" Joe Gallo's own photo album might today be innocently mistaken for a convention of polyester salesmen, but it was not so wrinkle-free a congregation that met in the weeks preceding Gallo's public execution. Above, Armando "Mando" Illiano plays party host while top Gallo aide Frank Illiano—seated third from left and reputedly as skillful in the kitchen as he was with his fists—plays it cool. Below, Peter "Pete the Greek" Diapoulas (inhaling) was Gallo's bodyguard during the fatal predawn shootout at Umberto's Clam House as well as the only person prosecuted in connection with the event—for possessing an unregistered firearm. His handgun was unloaded at the time of his arrest because his remaining live rounds had been cleverly emptied into the widow's handbag. (Both, author's collection.)

Armando "Mando" Illiano guides young Lisa Essary's hand as she slices into the first piece of birthday cake, while "Crazy" Joe Gallo (in newsboy cap) choreographs all the action. Illiano maintained a social club of his own, just down the block from the Gallo headquarters on President Street. Only a few weeks after this image was taken, Lisa would be compelled to witness Gallo being gunned down during his own birthday celebration. (Both, author's collection.)

Even while imprisoned for attempted extortion, "Crazy" Joe Gallo worked to maintain authority over gang members like Tony Bernardo (above, in vest), but his coded letters were confiscated by prison authorities. Bernardo was once arrested in front of the Manhattan District Attorney's Office, armed with a shotgun, while detectives escorted a whistleblower who said Gallo bragged of committing Albert Anastasia's barbershop murder. Below, Gallo's men (standing from left to right) Steven Cirillo, Bobby Darrow, Bobby Boriello, Toddo Marino, and Jimmy Springers gather around a .38 Special that, if nickel-plated steel could talk, would no doubt tilt the ear of New York City Rackets detectives. Three years after this portrait, Cirillo was presiding over "Vegas Nite" in the basement of a Brooklyn synagogue when a sniper's bullet killed him before 70 reluctant witnesses. (Author's collection.)

Undercover agents scrutinize mafia leader Joseph Columbo (far left, beside future government informant Joseph Cantalupo) whose bravado was such that his Italian-American Civil Rights League began picketing the FBI's Manhattan offices in May 1970 to protest what Columbo described as the government's prejudice against his specific ethnic group. Accompanying Columbo is bodyguard Rocco Miraglia (far right), an early suspect in "Crazy" Joe Gallo's murder; Gallo allegedly threw him from a second-story window shortly before the fatal shootout at Umberto's Clam House. Upon his parole, Gallo did not join Columbo's civil rights crusade; instead he renewed his Knights of Columbus membership (below) and demanded Columbo pay him a cash tribute. (Below, author's collection.)

KNIGHTS OF COLUMBUS

THIS IS TO CERTIFY THAT

BROTHER JOSEPH GALLO

MEMBER NO. IS A 3rd DEGREE MEMBER OF

COUNCIL NO. 585 BROOKLYN, NEW YORK

CITY STATE

DUES PAID TO Dec 31 1971

WILLIAM SPADAFINO G. K.

F. S.

Joey Gallo

MEMBER SIGNATURE

Modesto Santoro (above, in fedora) was a typical soldier in the family of Joseph Columbo when, in 1966, he invited a man police described as a prominent New York City building contractor on a boat ride in Brooklyn. Once out to sea, Santoro allegedly stripped the contractor bare and offered to throw him overboard if demands for cash were not met. Then in 1971, Santoro extorted $72,000 in small bills from the Mobil Oil Corporation, whose executives hired him to deliver gasoline during a labor strike, later admitting they had been aware of Santoro's reputation as a mobster but employed him anyway. Seen here participating in a Columbo picket line, "Strike Force Agent" Santoro and an associate identified as Pat Canterine (below) also seem eminently aware of the FBI agents in their midst. (Both, author's collection.)

Bookmakers mix with leg-breakers at the mob-controlled Latin Quarter nightclub in Manhattan. Seated third from the right is a young burglar named Joseph "Joe Yack" Yacovelli, who 20 years later was appointed leader of the Columbo organization and credited with dispatching the team

of gunmen that killed "Crazy" Joe Gallo on his 43rd birthday. Nativity was also a bad luck omen for the loan shark known as "Nicky Knock" (far left), who was fatally shot one Christmas Eve in front of St. Patrick's Church on Mulberry Street. (Author's collection.)

This is Umberto's Clam House as it appeared shortly after Columbo crime family gunmen ambushed "Crazy" Joe Gallo, who was dining here with his new wife and family on April 7, 1972. Visible is the Hester Street exit from which Gallo bolted before colliding with a similarly parked car. An unidentified man is passing over the precise spot where Gallo fell. (Author's collection.)

As "Crazy" Joe Gallo lay displayed in an open casket, NYPD detectives, who predicted bloody reprisals, observed the activities of his associates. Here Angelo Parfumi is a target of surveillance as he arrives to pay final respects at Guido's Funeral Home in Brooklyn, reputedly owned by the same crime family widely believed to have collected on Gallo's murder contract. (Author's collection.)

Motion picture director Abel Ferrara does his best Don Corleone impersonation and auditions the fedora worn by "Crazy" Joe Gallo the morning he died in Little Italy. Theories about Gallo's death are plentiful; some say revenge for a pastry shop burglary while others point to older scores, belatedly settled with bullets. Gallo had barely left prison when his executioners came calling. His birth and death intersected neatly, but even as he expired on asphalt, his legend lived and breathed in the streets of New York City. (Photograph by Arthur Nash; Brando silkscreen by Arthur Weinstein.)